Social Media
for
Baby Boomers

Social Media *for* Baby Boomers

How to translate your decades of knowledge
and experience into social influence

Sandra D'Souza

RƎTHINK PRESS

First published in Great Britain 2015
by Rethink Press (www.rethinkpress.com)

© Copyright Sandra D'Souza

Cover image © Little Whale, Shutterstock.com

Barry and Allegra, the loves of my life.

Mary, I have and will always love you.

Contents

Foreword

Forty is the new 30, and if you are in the over-40 category then this book is for you. The times in which we live are characterised by two almost diametrically opposed forces: the aging of the population and the embracing of technology by the young. How are we to reconcile this juxtaposition?

Although the baby boomer generation was one of change, if not revolution, it seems that the over-40s are failing to continue the embracing of change in the face of a larger than ever demand for such. The prevailing example of this need for change is the technology-driven march of social media and the associated search for social influence. With the wealth of experience that resides with mature age professionals (MaPs) there would appear to be a huge opportunity to leverage that experience to engage with and inform the masses (read "Gen X and Gen Y").

Being generally further along their career path means that MaPs have an even greater responsibility for being leaders in this new connected world. However, for various reasons the take-up of social media by executive and other senior MaPs is far less than in the community at large, and certainly well below that of Gen X and Gen Y. Those reasons might be inertia: "I've never had to do this before so why change?"; fear: "I don't know about this new technology"; ignorance: "I can't see the benefit"; or misunderstanding: "I don't have the time".

What these naysayer MaPs don't know is that social media leverage of their experience, knowledge, and skills can unlock opportunities for them that would otherwise go untapped.

Those opportunities include better meeting their employer's demands (e.g. for revenue growth), career development, career change, personal development, better management of younger staff, and for those self-employed, wider exposure of their services. There are also health benefits for the brain in acquiring new mental skills beyond the age of 40.

In my case it has been of substantial benefit in allowing me greater choice in my career path, which has provided higher financial rewards and higher personal satisfaction than would otherwise have been the case. It has also contributed to a high degree of success in my profession of sales and sales management. The stimulation I have gained by both participating in and engaging with prolific users of social media has been immense. Being a baby boomer myself and over the age of 60, I can attest that social media has kept me young in attitude and been a source of valuable insights into the lives and motivations of Gen Y, including my own children.

My story is not unique by any means, but based on quite a lot of anecdotal evidence it is unfortunately in the minority. I was an early adopter of social media back in January 2004 when I signed up on LinkedIn, thereby being one of the select first 100,000 members. Since that time I have taken up Facebook, Twitter, Google+ and other social media platforms. Each one for me has specific uses while also being part of a social media montage. That montage addresses an eclectic mix of personal, business, wider social, and sometimes combined needs for information exchange and, dare I say it, enlightenment.

The evolutionary path of my social media experiences has taken me into social selling, which I can best describe as the ability to utilise and leverage social media to enable willing, meaningful, and mutually beneficial engagement with prospective customers. This is not about "push" selling, nor is it about deceitful selling: it is about understanding buyers' needs and drivers and genuinely helping them to meet those needs. Surprisingly, that will sometimes result in you helping them to buy your competitor's product.

Coming back to the MaPs out there, unless you take up the call to become part of the social media "solution" to interconnectedness, you will sadly either be left behind and ignored, or even worse, pilloried for being part of the social media "problem" and told to get out of the way. Let's not forget the Luddites!

Sandra has clearly identified the issues and dependencies surrounding social media adoption by MaPs, the result of which is a succinct statement of the challenges, solution, and benefits to be gained by all, not least by the MaPs themselves. When I hear the quote attributed to Mahatma Gandhi to "be the change you wish to see in the world" I recognise that there has never been a time in history when we were better equipped to do that, given the reach of social media.

I hope you enjoy the book.

Steve Walker

Steve Walker is a successful senior executive who has been operating in the IT industry for the last 20 years. With a background that saw him as one of the featured entrepreneurs in Creating Entrepreneurs *by Denise Fleming, published by Allen and Unwin, 1988, Steve has become a leading sales strategist. An early pioneer in the concept of social selling, Steve is a full-time Sales Manager as well as sitting on a number of advisory boards to IT start-ups.*

Introduction

I started peeling my clothes off in the train carriage during a morning peak hour trip to the city because I was trying to stop myself from passing out. I was drenched in sweat, my synthetic hair wig was clinging on to my head, and I yearned to find a free seat as my legs were getting close to giving way. I clung on as long as I could to get to my stop, then headed out as quickly as possible once the doors opened to the seat bench on the platform and lay across it. The cool air soothed my hotness and the stillness of the bench calmed every cell in my body until I could sit up again.

That was one of my hardest days during my chemotherapy treatment.

I often get the surprised look from friends and colleagues as to why I was still working while I was being treated for breast cancer. Probably because I felt well enough, I love doing what I do, and I could physically get up each day and face the world. I learned this from my six-year-old daughter who has battled to stay alive ever since she was born, with her frequent and extensive hospital admissions. She's already had nearly two dozen near death experiences, and every time she recovers, she comes home with a bigger smile and achieves further progress over her physical disabilities. She has a lot of reasons to complain about the unfairness in her life and the struggles she endures, but instead she offers unconditional love to those around her and commitment to overcoming her daily struggles.

Inspired by her, I have decided to write this book while I'm going through chemotherapy because I want to show you that managing your social media profiles is actually easy and does not have to be scary or time consuming. It is often our innate fear that stops us from embracing new approaches and we come up with many reasons why we don't want to embrace it. This book will address them in detail, and I hope that by sharing with you my personal story first that you will overcome your hesitation and start to learn how to develop your social media influence, as the world needs you and wants you to impart your decades of professional experience and knowledge to them.

Why Age Is Not A Barrier To Your Social Media Influence

You've been a mature working professional for a number of years. Many changes in customer and client communication, brand-management, and advertising have naturally evolved over the course of your career. You've seen hot new innovations come and go, and not all of them have applied to you or your business model. However, the most dramatic communications shift in recent history has unquestionably been the global cultural acceptance of social media. All signs indicate social media isn't on its way out. It's a part of your work experience you simply can't afford to skip out on.

In the early years of social media (once known by the outdated term "Web 2.0") it was common corporate practice to assign a digital guru to handle all of an organisation's social media communication needs. Those days are past. It's become every professional's responsibility to embrace these platforms as a means of improving both internal and external communications. If you don't control your message, social media has been designed to let your audience control that message for you. It has become an essential professional and management tool to embrace and understand. Modern professionals need to learn social communications in order to improve relations with their employees, clients, and public.

At this point, it might be reasonable to ask the question, why? If you've been accustomed to growing your professional networks and business through more traditional means and it's still working for you, there may be some natural reticence to investing your already limited professional hours into technology that's not as clearly established.

If you're still not convinced that social media is the best use of your time or that it's just a tool that's meant for the younger workforce to play with, you're passing up on an opportunity to connect in a profoundly meaningful way. You already have a lifetime of experiences and invaluable knowledge to share with that same generation. There's no one better equipped to be a powerful influencer through social media than the mature professional.

I manage a successful digital marketing agency. Being a mature-aged person, I personally understand and can relate to your concerns, but I've got great news to share with you: social media is far more intuitive than you may realise. There's absolutely no reason to miss out on the many benefits of social media simply because of perceived technological barriers or fears of appearing narcissistic.

If you think you've got no one your age to share this adventure with, you're wrong. Our generation is already more involved in social media than you may think. According to the Nielson

Report, there's a large percentage of the Baby Boomer generation already involved in the Australian online community: 6.3 million Boomers were online in the month of March 2015[1].

Did you know that among Australian Baby Boomers online:

- 37.5% visited Facebook, representing almost a fifth of all page views
- 27% were more likely to have visited the professional networking platform LinkedIn during 2015 than peers in other age groups.[2]

I realise you probably aren't new to the *idea* of social media, and I'm not planning to provide a 101 step-by-step approach to understanding the detailed specifics of the technology or individual platforms such as Twitter, Facebook, or Pinterest. Social media moves fast and it's better to learn the individual platforms in a more focused context. Instead, I want to address the issues that are preventing you from fully benefiting from this interactive digital medium directly. I'll present the arguments for why you should be excited about the new era of communications and how it can benefit your career and your organisation. Then we'll address eight common concerns that might be holding you back.

After we've reviewed the pros and cons, there's a five step process I'm going to share with you for setting yourself up for success in your social media endeavours. We'll conclude by reviewing the six golden rules: a set of helpful hints for fully engaging in the experience and to help guide you as a respected social communicator.

[1] Nielsen Online Ratings, March 2015

[2] Nielsen Online –Hybrid, March 2015

Social media isn't just a flash in the pan. It's here to stay, and this is the way your audience expects to receive information from you. Though it's a learning process, it's also an art you can learn as you go. You may think you don't have what it takes to accomplish much in this realm. It's not true. Don't worry, you have decades of experience to draw upon that will serve you well here.

If you haven't heard this from anyone else yet, I want to be the first to welcome you to the art of social storytelling. You've got important, valuable stories to share. Let's get you ready to connect with and become a strong social mentor for younger audiences and your already connected peers.

Section 1

Why You Should Use Social Media

If you don't think you engage in social media right now, I have news for you: you actually do. Your absence has been noted by employees and clients. In case you don't realise the ways you're missing out by not actively engaging in this world, let me tell you the three ways that setting aside your fears and diving into the social media world can directly benefit you.

Chapter 1

Embrace Social Media, Don't Fear It

I may be wrong in your specific case, but I have a feeling you've probably already sat through a presentation or two regarding why you should be using social media. After you've been earnestly walked through the various slides and shown the data by an excited proponent of the technology, you've had questions answered and had a chance to weigh your options. You've likely been asked to come down on the side of a yes or no for moving forward. If you're still weighing the decision or reconsidering it, please allow me to tell you the right answer.

The right answer is a definitive yes.

I'm not trying to tell you how to run your business. I'm solely interested in helping you see that, as a mature professional, you're missing out on a wealth of opportunities. The overwhelming reason you may have decided to opt out, I believe, has to do with fear.

I've felt it myself. Who hasn't been confronted with an unfamiliar technology and, while struggling to determine how it works and how it will benefit them, has simply decided to walk away? It's a natural response.

Yet, if you look at the social media landscape today, there are no major business interests left who aren't engaged in some way with social media. Take a look at the top biggest Australian businesses. BHP Billiton, National Australia Bank, Commonwealth Bank, Rio Tinto Group, ANZ, Westpac, Telstra, Macquarie Bank, and AMP represent nine of the ten largest Australian businesses as of May 2015, and all nine are on Twitter.

Woolworths, the only one of the ten not actively tweeting, does have an active Facebook page and Instagram account. It also has an inactive Twitter account, and even without Woolworths engaging with its clients on Twitter, those clients are talking about them.

If you're not familiar with the concept, on Twitter one can use a hashtag to post a topic. Anyone searching for that topic will find similar conversations. There were 104 discussions revolving around #Woolworths between 1 May and 23 May. Some of those comments were negative. By not being there, the company wasn't able to engage with those unhappy customers and respond to their concern.

According to *The Telegraph*[1], the average audience for each Twitter user in 2012 was 208 followers. That's a potential reach of 21,632 people just from the tag #Woolworths. Consider that retweeting – that is, sharing – a Twitter post can exponentially grow the potential audience for a single negative tweet. One negative tweet was shared 62 times.

I hope you are starting to see my point. Simply not getting involved is always an option, but it isn't necessarily a great one. If large-scale operations are invested in social media, there's

---

[1] "Average Twitter user is an American woman with an iPhone and 208 followers", *The Telegraph*, 11 October 2012. Website, 23 May 2015.

good reason to consider why your endeavour should be proactive in taking on these discussions.

Let's talk about the two faces of social media. Just like nearly all of your business communications (with the exception of possibly collaborative communications) the bulk of your existing information sharing is conducted internally or externally.

External Social Media

When we speak of external social media, we're talking about an audience consisting of your clients, partners, and the general public. This is how your organisation does business. Whatever its purpose, for profit or non-profit, your organisation can't exist in a void and benefits by seeking connections with these folks. Therefore, you're going to have to deal with a certain amount of back and forth on a regular basis.

Because businesses tend to think externally, social media has a higher profile in this arena. We already know we need to keep communications pathways open for the outside; we may just choose to focus how those communications are pipelined in. That can lead to reduced interactions and an unchallenged negative public perception in certain communities, as shown in the earlier example.

Beyond considering the negative elements, there's the positive to think about as well. Who better to champion your brand in these untapped markets than you? As a mature professional, your experience in the business is of immense value in evangelising to new customers and partners around your particular brand. There's no better way to build the respect of your colleagues than to share useful information freely and generously.

Apart from simply sharing your latest deals and acquisitions, don't forget that social media can be an excellent way to manage crisis communications. Through the collaborative nature of social media, it's quite possible to address a situation that may arise directly and expect that answer to be shared to numerous users.

While we'll address it more in-depth later on, your role as a leader in this area is vital. Don't worry about appearing "narcissistic". If you're a subject matter expert with deep knowledge of your area of expertise, trust me – people will want to hear your voice.

Internal Social Media

If you happen to work in Human Resources, this is essentially where you live. It's vital to your workforce productivity that messages are received clearly and acted upon professionally. If your organisation isn't able to negotiate its own internal messaging shortcomings, it'll be obvious to the rest of the world in no time.

Internal social media doesn't have the same profile as external social media and is unfortunately one of the more overlooked areas of corporate communication development. Challenges in this area include adapting the culture to acceptance of this tool, maintaining long-term interest, and drawing in leadership to champion and participate actively in the tool. This is where we mature professionals need to set the tone and lead.

Internal social media is quite helpful within larger organisations where people may not interact on a regular basis, if at all. Suddenly, all of your employees have the ability to exchange collaborative documents, informational links, and personal knowledge openly with anyone else within the organisation.

Naturally, that could lead to headaches, not unlike when email was introduced into corporate culture. Whenever information is shared, there's the potential for confidential or draft materials to be disseminated. However, internal social media is a little different from the anything-goes anonymous threats existing in the wider digital world.

Consider that every person involved within an internal social media network will be easily identifiable; there's no anonymity in such tools, meaning that anyone using the network should be expected to maintain the same degree of professionalism as they would with their normal communication channels. Depending on the scale of your organisation, you may want to designate a community leader or two to help monitor internal discussions. Very likely these will be the same people who set up and maintain the normal running of the platform, but they could just as easily be individuals who establish themselves as excellent community sharers.

What if there are major changes coming to the workplace? Rather than just notifying your employees through a string of workshops, flyers, and emails, consider that the campaign could be shared through internal social media. The point person for those changes could update staff regarding progress towards the move to a new location or major developments in a procurement process, for example.

Internal social media offers one more important long-lasting benefit that can also be overlooked. With employee turnover comes a loss in knowledge. Yet with these platforms, it's entirely possible to tag and archive that knowledge so that when anyone searches on a topic (let's say #VacationPolicy or #LeavePolicy) it doesn't matter if the established expert on that policy is by chance on holidays. The organisation's knowledge – including your own – can be retained and considered for new employees down the road.

I mentioned crisis communications in the external example. Consider also that emergency and crisis communications handled via social media internally can be extremely beneficial. It may be one of the first places your employees go for notifications regarding workplace closures or natural disasters.

Where do you fit in with both these internal and external programs? In the lead, of course. Mature professionals who support and engage in social media themselves build confidence in the entire organisation in that undertaking.

You've been doing much the same thing for decades in other areas of the organisation. Why should social media be any different?

Chapter 2

Social Media Is As Essential As Having An Email Account

It's easy to fall into the trap of thinking of social media as simply being another information delivery system, like your web page, fax, or email. A common early era mistake for new entrants jumping into the medium was to do nothing more than share ad campaigns and post press releases. While there are overlaps between the medium and web development, interaction plays a starring role in social media. Social media networking has evolved far beyond the old "Web 2.0" definition.

Depending on your organisation and its goals, it can still be important and effective to share materials like press releases. However, if your communications feed is cluttered with nothing but one-way messaging, you're likely to be turning off your audience. They'll learn to tune out.

Email is a good two-way communications method, but it has its limitations. We've all come back from vacation with the knowledge that we face a mountain of inbox slush to wade through. While clearing out your inbox, you may inadvertently sweep out all the group emails that share interesting but not essential information with you. Professional groups may be trying to connect with you, but who has time when you're busy dealing with managing your staff and keeping the higher-ups satisfied?

Social media platforms are designed to organise and catalogue your interests better for you. You can stay connected with professional development groups, interacting when your time permits. In the same way clients expect information to come to them in the way they want, you can benefit by setting priorities within your own networks, both internal and external.

Obviously, social media can't and shouldn't replace your email. Instead, it should serve to augment your information infrastructure. It allows you to declutter your inbox so that only those items that need to be there are waiting for you when you sit down at your desk.

Public enquiry isn't a new field, and professionals have been handling incoming requests for information for a long time. You may worry about how these new media developments will impact public enquiry. The transition is actually fairly simple. If you set up a good system for capturing incoming information and relaying it to your subject matter experts for responses, enquiry handling needn't be any more complex than how you already respond to phone calls. We'll go into more detail on how to plan for that later on in Section 3.

There's another consideration to be aware of, and while it's applicable to external audiences, it's particularly relevant to internal audiences. Your workforce is necessarily changing. The way they receive and engage with information is an important part of keeping pace with that change.

As I'm sure you're aware, Baby Boomers aren't the only players in the workforce. As of 2015, there are three major groups to consider across the workforce spectrum: those of us born between 1946 and 1964, the Baby Boomer generation; Generation X, born between 1965 and 1980; and Generation Y, a group born between 1981 and 1995. The terms aren't perfect, of course, and the years aren't really all that hard and fast, so while these artificial constructs for thinking of people by age group are useful for better understanding generational thinking, these are loosely defined categories and by no means representative of every individual member.

It should be noted that the fourth generation of workers, Generation Z, isn't well understood yet, considering the oldest of those workers are just now entering the workforce. However, we do know that they've grown up never knowing a world without text messaging or social media. It's a consideration worth planning for in the years ahead.

If you're communicating with any of these four generations solely by email, you're doing a disservice to your own message. Outside of work, all four workforce generations are connecting to their favourite communities through social media. Email, while a -useful and important communications tool, is no substitute for the ability to influence and share knowledge through less hierarchical structures found in social media communities. The expectation is already there. You need to be where your employees would expect to find you.

Memos and emails support hierarchies. For an organisation, there's certainly a place for that kind of structure and workflow. However, there are going to be times when, as a leader, you want feedback from your employees. More than that, you want to make sure that all of your employees are networking with each other in the most efficient way possible. You may find that an important question can be answered by the person you least expect within your organisation. It may be that the person who says the least in meetings has the most valuable information to impart through online networking. That's where an internal social media presence can pay dividends.

Don't be discouraged if you still think this is for your workers, not necessarily for you. It's a cool new world for mature workers in this environment as well. Your most recent hire may have knowledge to share in their particular skill set, but no one has the breadth of experience to impart that we mature professionals can offer. When you were moving up through the ranks, you almost certainly had a mentor or two who took you under their wing. Imagine having the ability to play a respected mentoring role to an entire community of your colleagues on a regular basis. It's not as time-consuming a role as you might imagine.

While these principles apply to internal communications, they're vital to connecting with your clients as well. There was a time when salespeople found the best way to connect with a decision-maker was to make an appointment, drive to their place of business, sit down at their office, and make their pitch. Over time, phone calls and emails became a more cost-effective means of pitching, though that could involve bothersome filtering through office administrators, unanswered voicemail, or the recipient simply failing to open the email.

Social media works differently. Instead of booking time with the decision-maker, you're invited to become a part of your client's self-selected pre-screened business network. So long as you're providing value in your communications, they're going to remain interested in what you have to say.

None of this innovation renders the previous communications approaches obsolete. When entertainment transitioned from radio to television, and later began to move from television to online subscriptions, the previous mediums didn't cease to exist. People will always have an individual preference for how they want to communicate. Whether that's by chat, phone, face-to-face, teleconferencing, or online bulletin boards, all forms are still relevant.

However, social media's ability to overcome filters and hierarchies has built powerful, flexible systems that aren't platform dependent. It doesn't really matter which "type" of social media you choose to engage in. If you've heard of Friendster or MySpace, you already know the market dominance of a particular platform can shift overnight. This is a good thing. The platforms are constantly changing to suit the needs of the global user. The same principles of "innovate or die" that fuel business dynamics drive the need for better user experiences.

That's why social media as a broad concept is so non-specific when it comes to platforms. Not everyone is going to be comfortable framing their ideas in 140 characters or less. For them, it may be better to connect with their brands and communities through a Facebook group or a Tumblr page. They may choose to share photos on Pinterest, check out videos on YouTube, and yet find those same videos on a Google+ page. Two years from now when we look back at this chapter, we may even find a few of those names are no longer relevant. When users define their experiences, platforms are forced to react or give ground to competition.

If I've scared you further with all the name references, don't worry. The main point is that social media is flexible. So long as you're flexible as well, you have nothing to worry about. Your audience is out there. Connect with it!

Chapter 3

People Can Get To Know The Real You Through Social Media

Have you ever worried that your public persona is being misunderstood? Afraid you're not getting your point across effectively?

Your personal image may not be your greatest concern when you have a complicated organisation to manage. Yet, having a positive and relatable image is a key element in recruiting allies when they're needed, in building goodwill for campaigns, and for effectively dealing with PR crisis communication situations that may naturally arise.

If you're choosing to avoid social media because you don't want to see the business overly focused on you, it's important to realise that your presence can be an effective way of growing your connections directly to people so they'll better understand the real you beneath the decisions you make. Believe it or not, people are interested.

Your image reflects upon the organisation you work for, whether you wish it or not. A lack of public image can be every bit as damaging as a negative one in the age of social media. It's important to know how to make your public self help you out with your career and your business.

There's a reason people follow celebrities on platforms like Twitter. Successful Twitter communicators grow their following by engaging directly with their followers. They take their message straight to their people, friends, and fans, and when the people speak, they listen and respond directly. Even though the connection may be brief, it does remind followers and fans that the people they're interested in are human, just like them.

Allow me to provide an example. I've done some work with up-and-coming authors in the past. One related to me a good story about how a small gesture can be a big deal to people on Twitter.

My author friend was unpublished at the time, and had put out a tweet indicating that he intended to share an excerpt from his upcoming novel. A few people liked his tweet, but what really caught his attention was a like from a publishing executive's personal account. The executive happened to work in fiction at one of the major publishing houses. This didn't mean the publisher wanted to see the author's work or even read the excerpt; the executive had just given him the equivalent of a thumbs up for his strategy and tweet. My friend related this account to me, and you'd think he'd already been signed with a huge advance, the positive feedback meant that much to him.

The author realised the limit of the engagement, so it wasn't an instance of the like giving a misleading signal. It was just a way of interacting on a level that was meaningful and overcame the normal barriers of bottlenecks and appointments.

The celebrity-fan relationship needn't be any different for an executive. Celebrities, for their personal safety and privacy, do need to maintain some layers between themselves and the public, and that's understandable. The same is true of the executive. However, as soldiers in combat have related in countless war stories, the generals who were willing to sit down and eat with the troops, who took an interest in their wellbeing, and who made an effort to relate to their hardships and struggles were often the leaders for whom soldiers bore a special affection. That loyalty can only come from genuine connections.

You don't need to become a social media celebrity to have an impact, nor do you need to be a corporate celebrity before you step into the role of online educator and leader. All you need to do to introduce yourself is to find the conversations where your voice is welcome and to speak. Having a platform or two is only a beginning: it's a handshake or a resume. It's not the interview and it's not the daily process of accomplishing great things that help you stand out. Having those platforms is a help, but it's not as important as getting out there and sharing your wisdom with others.

What if you're worried the worst aspects of your personality are going to shine through in social media? Honestly, experience is a fine teacher in this respect. If you're already aware of your shortcomings, simply work to harness them to your advantage on social media, just as you've done in your personal and professional life.

If you tend to be shy, social media is your friend. You don't have to be in anyone's physical presence or speak out loud to be heard. Take your time and write what you want to say, if you don't plan to step in front of a camera. Your voice will carry in a neutral fashion if you pay attention to online etiquette. Anyone who happens across your post can learn from you.

If you find you tend to get overheated and emotional in conversations, no problem. As I like to say, it's okay to take a deep breath and disengage from time to time. Take a step back! There's never a hurry to rush into unhappy conversations on social media. Use it when your head is clear and your heart is open to listen.

Perhaps you have a tendency to talk too much. No problem. Take a look at the words you're writing. If you have to break them into more than 140 characters, don't tweet. If you need to share more than two paragraphs, don't do it over Facebook. If you have more than a Word page to write – well, more like two-thirds of a Word page, let's say – you shouldn't blog. Instead, save that write-up for your webpage and link back to it from your social media accounts.

The point is, use these human frailties to your communications advantage by consciously appraising where you can work to improve your message.

You didn't get where you are by failing to show tremendous leadership skills. There's no doubt that connecting on internal social media and directly engaging with your employees will help to establish connections. When budgets are tight and raises hard to come by, employees may feel more loyalty to the executive who praised them for their prompt responses to questions, their strong ideas, or the examples they're setting within the community. A little bit of praise goes a long way.

You may be tempted to delegate the bulk of your personal social media. Let me give you a word of caution there. It's important to have social media professionals working for you, but they can't *be* you. Nor should you want them to be.

One thing I can't emphasise enough: don't have other people write personal communications for you on social media. That's not to say you can't or shouldn't get help in developing your ideas for different platforms. For instance, if you're going to write a blog, it's okay if someone else is writing the contextual text for links to the blog from social media platforms. There's nothing wrong with farming out a smaller-scale communication if it's essentially an announcement.

A blog is an excellent way to get your voice out there, in particular to share your expertise with others. When you establish a blog, you may have the option to close off comments – don't do it! The comments are where the questions come in that you are best suited to answer. Be sure you monitor the blog and answer anything that comes up. It's essential that you don't ignore the opportunity to communicate with your fans.

There are some things that can only be effectively communicated by being genuine. The back and forth of social media encourages honesty in your communications. It develops bonds and trust in relationships. Because of the size of the communities we touch, it may initially be that you feel your voice is drowned out. Don't worry! You have maturity and patience on your side. When you speak, others will listen because what you have to say is of value. Expect to bring that to your conversations, and in this way make a strong difference with your listeners.

Despite your experience, if you are noted as a person who's willing to learn from others and listen, your respect in the community can only be improved.

Hopefully, I've been able to convince you there are several benefits to taking part in social media. If you're still undecided, allow me to tackle some of the reasons you may still be holding back.

Section 2

Eight Reasons Why You Are Not Active On Social Media For Your Business

There are plenty of excuses for not taking an active role in your organisation's social media efforts. Let's explore those justifications and consider how they're holding back your potential.

Chapter 4

Fear Of Using Technology

I get it. Social media and technology aren't part of your comfort zone. We all have ways we like to communicate, and you're afraid this may not be one of them for you.

Guess what – the companies who built social media understand that fear as well. They're well aware that there are plenty of other options for you and me to connect with our kids, grandkids, and friends. That's why they've gone to great lengths to design their platforms to be as easy to use as possible.

While I may say that, it's not always the case that every element of these tools appears easy to jump right into. After all, it is your first time using the platform, and some of them (like Facebook, for instance) have many features that can be visually confusing at first. However, if you create an account and proceed into the main area of any of the most adopted platforms, one of the first things you'll encounter is a field that encourages you to type or upload something in there. They want you to start making and sharing things right away.

Each platform is going to have its rules to abide by, and you'll learn them with experience. For example, Twitter has a 140 character limit, and that includes spaces and links. You have to plan your messages accordingly. For Facebook, that limit as of May

2015 was 63,206 characters. If you maxed that out, that'd be around 10,000 words, or one-third the size of this book, which is a pretty long post! Regardless of the limits or the kind of content, the idea behind social media is that you develop compelling content that others want to engage in.

That's right. You're just creating content, and that shouldn't be a new experience for most of us. If you've been a communicator for many of your professional years, this is not so different from what you've already been doing all along. It's just another format, like the progression from typewriter to computer to smartphone. The technology may not be all that comfortable, but it's still accomplishing the same goal: to share.

When it comes to managing the details of the technology, it may be useful to you if you have a social media strategist, social media manager, or community manager to work within your organisation. If you do not have a budget to hire such experts, then you can outsource to a digital marketing agency like Curate Bee Digital which can provide you the expertise across a spectrum of skills at a fraction of the cost of a full-time hire. Either way, I'll be discussing those roles later in the book, but you can see them as roughly analogous to those of your web development, PR, or print communications teams.

However, it's important to note that most of those roles often overlap into other jobs. It's quite possible that your web development head will also be your social media strategist, in particular if you have a well-trained digital media team. Whatever way you choose to structure this layout, realise that it's perfectly fine to have staff who act as your point people. Even as they act as the evangelists, trainers, strategists, and community go-tos, though, you need to trust that everyone on your staff is going to have to figure out social media to some extent, in particular if they are executives or communicators. If not, appoint a digital marketing or social media agency to help you to navigate the technology and social media strategy.

If your primary goal is to establish a personal presence, whether it's a blog or a Twitter account, or simply sharing photos and highlights from conferences you've attended, most of the technical backend can be farmed out while you focus on messaging. How difficult is it to tailor your messaging for social media? It's not hard at all if you're already used to communicating in more traditional ways. The skills carry over.

A key element to consider is the fact that you should be brief when possible. That can be a change if you're used to communicating in more formal language, but think of it as just trying to convey the main idea to your audience. Most of the time, you'll need to link to a webpage or an online form to relay further information – yes, you do still have to maintain a web presence on top of social media! Whereas the web is a bit more static than social media, it is an excellent place for conveying greater detail or allowing your audience to take further steps through a call-to-action. I'll have more tips for you later.

If you can't afford to take the step of assigning people to handle your technical issues, or if you've suddenly found yourself appointed to fill one of those roles, there's no cause for alarm. As previously mentioned, social media technology is fairly simple to figure out. If you're creating a corporate presence, most of the platforms will allow you to create pages (organisational presence) as opposed to profiles (your personal presence). The names may vary or the platform (such as Twitter) may not make a distinction. If you have to do something like this, it's usually just a simple matter of setting goals, planning, setup, ongoing review, and tweaking the work. We'll cover those specifics more in Section 3.

In the meantime, I want you to consider how, over your many decades as a business professional, you've been asked to learn emerging technologies. We've seen innovations rise and surpass our previous comfortable ways of doing things. It's not a conspiracy of the young over the mature; it's the natural pattern of life. If you think about how successful you've been leading up to this point in your life, it's much less intimidating to take on this challenge.

You've got a lifetime of experience to draw on for your storytelling through this medium. Amazingly, you're likely to have more stories to tell about your own flexibility and adaptability than the other generations of workers in your workplace; you've had far more experience with new things than your younger cohorts. So no fear! You can surely conquer this experience as well.

Let's continue tackling fear by discussing another common complaint: a lack of time.

Chapter 5

No Time To Maintain Actively

"I have endless meetings, strategies to review, a full schedule. It might be I could squeeze something in, but I don't see how I can keep this thing going with all that I'm already expected to do. Same with my workforce. It's just one more thing on my plate."

You may be trying to make the case that your time is limited. In doing so, you may well be overlooking the time-consuming things you do each and every day. Social media can actually help you get better control over these issues, if put to good use. These platforms can be a great way to displace less effective communications.

If you're already doing the following things:

- Writing emails and letters to staff
- Writing emails and letters to clients
- Responding to enquiries
- Holding staff meetings to share updates
- Making plans to meet with clients
- Developing advertising for television or radio
- Developing training
- Mentoring younger employees

you've got time for social media.

Every business requires a certain amount of effort be put into communication, whether it's internal or external. If you're taking calls from clients who are voicing concerns about how your proposed new structure will impact the environment, aren't you saving both you and the client time by researching those concerns through social media? The worries are probably already being discussed and can be addressed in this way. Perhaps the problem can even be avoided entirely.

One thing that's not going to happen: the newer workforce generations aren't going to communicate outside of work using the older technologies, and they're not going to expect to go back to the days of fax, inter-office mail, and stickies as their sole sources of information. Most professionals have a smartphone in their pockets. You should expect they're going to communicate using the apps and social media most readily at hand: the ones they're most comfortable using.

It's time to think about this differently. You're always going to spend time at work. Now it's time to use it to communicate with a new mindset.

The reality is that social media isn't an extra time constraint in your communications efforts. Yes, the start-up and training will take a little time, in particular the time it takes to adjust. You already made a similar adjustment from hand-written memos to emails, didn't you? It wasn't always smooth, but eventually it became the leading way in which you did business. It's unlikely social media will take over your entire communications process. It is far more likely to become a new avenue for routing a particular type of communication, freeing up other things for better use.

Like email, checking your social media can be just another thing you do during the course of the day. Yes, you do have many intrusions into your time and I understand that can be unnerving, but as I mentioned, if people come to expect they can reach you over Facebook or Twitter rather than by a phone call, that may become the natural way of doing business. It has the advantage of being controllable as well. You may check social media every day; you don't have to check it every minute of the day.

If there are great links coming into your inbox for email, you may be tempted to toss them straight into recycle. However, for most social media, you can simply bookmark them for later reading. When you have some down time specifically for catching up on new developments, then you can scan your bookmarks for those links you couldn't read earlier.

You can also organise your topics by subject. It may be that instead of reading your Twitter account and trying to follow all the discussions the people you follow are talking about, you'd be better served simply to read a very specific hashtag. This will help you distil down the information you're bringing in and get you to the point a lot quicker.

When it comes to posting, there are many tools designed to allow you to craft your messaging and then release that information in a timed manner. Do you want to share an important post on a Sunday, but don't want to work that day? Not a problem. Use a scheduling tool to set the time for the release. You can usually use a scheduler across multiple platforms. Some platforms have a scheduler built right into the interface.

We'll discuss personnel later, but this campaign may be compatible with some of your more digitally-minded employees. It may not be such a major stretch to integrate a degree of maintenance into the work of a few of these employees. Rebalance as necessary, but you may find that a lot of the work that was previously being done by your print marketers should be redirected to this effort anyway.

What about training? Training does take time. The great thing about social media is that it's very likely you have people in your workforce who are actively involved in it outside of work. The systems they need to use for their jobs are the exact same systems and platforms they already use. If they're a little different, they won't be vastly different.

As social media continues to shift and evolve, your training happens on the job each and every day. You don't have to invest time by learning beyond the initial start-up. You're actively learning. So the time constraints aren't as severe as you might think. For example, at Curate Bee Digital, we are passionate about using great tools to be efficient in communicating so we use Newz Social. We use it to curate content, write content for posting as well as getting our clients to approve with ease through their own login the work we have planned for them. Their iphone and ipad App is free so I recommend you use it to help systemise and manage your sharing of your social media content.

Those same people who are most comfortable with social media already may be your best people to elevate to positions of responsibility within your social media networks. So long as they can distinguish personal use from company use, they're going to make excellent leaders in your effort and can help to manage cultural shifts towards the use of these platforms.

Finally, you will have a few people in your organisation (perhaps yourself?) who aren't at all comfortable with these technologies and who need a little extra help. Don't be shy about approaching the folks in your organisation that you've already tasked with social media responsibilities. They may be very eager to share their information with you – just ask!

We've addressed the pressure to make the best use of your time. Our next stop on the worries and excuses list is to address the pressure you may feel to perform well with the time you invest in social media.

Chapter 6

Feel Pressured To Do Really Well So Easier Not To Do It

"We're doing fine with what we've got. I know everyone else is out there on social media and the world is moving in that direction. Still, I'm not unhappy with the way things are. I don't think the investment, training, and resources are worth our time. I'll focus on other things."

It may be that you're feeling a lot of pressure to do social media simply for the sake of doing it. I would agree that one of the worst reasons to do something is because you're feeling pressured. A new effort isn't necessarily a good thing to get involved in just because people are telling you that you ought to.

What's more, if you think you have to do the best possible job in entering this area of communications to be successful, it may become a matter of just letting the opportunity pass you by. It's easier not to act and let events unfold on their own.

I wonder, though, is this how you've built your business and career so far? Did you wait for opportunities to pass you by and then go on doing what you'd been doing, ignoring changing trends because they were too much effort? I didn't think so! You're still working, so clearly this is not your usual way of doing things. Don't make social media the exception in your track record of successes.

Waiting for that perfect moment before you act? The perfect moment is now.

Listen: you don't have to be perfect at using social media and making social media platforms work to get started. Everyone starts off as a novice, and everyone you interact with on social media will understand that you're just getting started when you make connections. It's okay.

You're going to make a few mistakes in social media, and that's to be expected. You can best mitigate that by building a strong team, supporting them, and developing a reputation for sharing, caring, and honesty in your campaigns. Continue to practise the suggestions I'll provide in this book and take the initiative to continue your training as you go. Eventually you'll have exactly what you were looking for from your social media presence.

The only real mistake you can make is to let things lie because of fear of accomplishing less than excellence.

If you put off a decision, the decision is going to be made for you. By choosing not to engage in social media, you've actually made a choice to cut yourself off from opportunity, engagement, and untapped wealth of knowledge. You've also limited access to yourself and your knowledge, and that can create an unnecessary bottleneck.

How can you take some of the pressure off? There are a few ways I can suggest.

I'd begin by lurking. That sounds a bit ominous, doesn't it? It's really not. It's a term used to describe active users of social media platforms who don't contribute. Instead, they spend their time reading other postings and trying to gather information. Social media, by definition, is ideally social. It's best to put into the networks you're connected with. At the same time, that's not the way everyone interacts. Some users are more comfortable observing rather than posting.

This is okay as a way to get started. Before you get too involved in a social media platform, you can usually simply opt to lurk. Watch what you see. How are your customers, partners, and peers posting? Do you get a good sense of the community values from watching the interactions? Is it clear who the community leaders are, and are they necessarily the same individuals who are identified as the leaders? You can learn a tremendous amount from this approach, and it may help put you at ease a little more before formally joining the community.

Ah, but the time to lurk and the time to engage must at some point converge. You will actually need to pull the trigger and get into social media. What do you do if you still feel pressured?

I'd suggest you pick a single social media platform and ease your way into it. After you've done all of the five steps identified later on in this book, that launch process needn't be intense. You can start slowly and work your way up. By focusing on one platform and doing a "soft launch" as opposed to a full assault, you may gradually acclimatise yourself to this endeavour.

Lastly, realise that the five step process has a built-in safety measure for step five – tweaking and refining. Yes, you'll need to stay active and operational on a regular basis. But as you progress, you always have the option to change up your style. If something isn't working, fine. Let it go. Move on to something else.

I've worked with at least one organisation in the past that was using ecards as a communications approach. Initially, it seemed like a great outreach effort. They customised the ecards with specific messages and awesome graphics. Then they allowed website visitors to send those ecards out to their friends and families. The results for some initiatives were effective. Over time, returns began to diminish. They eventually disengaged that program, focusing on building up their presence on image-sharing social media platforms instead, such as Pinterest, Flickr, and Instagram. It was a necessary transition, and it's what worked for them.

Eventually, those platforms may go away, passing the way of eight-track players and arcade machines. That'll be fine. The processes and policies put in place are far more important than the specific platforms. After all, you're not still using MS-DOS, are you? If you're using a computer operating system, it's going to be a modern version (ideally), and you're going to be fairly comfortable using it because you've built on knowledge acquired from previous versions.

So you see, there's really no "pressure" per se. Don't let your fear of perfection prevent you from trying social media. Nothing is engraved in granite online. Yes, your messages may find some degree of permanence in some form or fashion. The question is, will they be relevant to the immediate audience? No one is going to think you're the worst company in the world if you send out a tweet with a typo in it. Obviously, avoid that practice whenever possible, but when it happens, delete the tweet and send out a correction if necessary. It's that simple.

If you've built up a degree of trust within a community, they'll accept your small errors the same way you should be expected to forgive theirs.

But perhaps you have a different problem. Maybe you've already tried social media and it's going wrong.

Chapter 7

Not Getting Results After A Lot Of Effort

"We gave it a try. I hired a dedicated digital guru and we signed up for a few accounts. I even tried writing a blog myself to share my thoughts. We did all we could and we're not seeing a lot of ROI on this thing. I'm ready to pull the plug."

You've already invested in social media and it's agreed: your efforts were a flop. Maybe you don't think you're drawing in enough followers and fans. Perhaps you have an audience, but it's not the one you want. I can understand that you'd want to stop.

It's fine to stop, meet with your social media staff or agency, and reconsider what you're doing – to a certain extent. Important components of social media include experimentation and flexibility. If you've tried a particular communications path and it's not working, it is the right move to reconsider your approach immediately.

The wrong move would be running away. How often do you work on a project and simply toss everything aside the moment it stops working? Practically never, right? At the very least, your organisation will be required to assess all the steps that took place. It's necessary to uncover which lessons you can learn so as not to repeat them in similar projects down the road.

We've established social media's not working for you. What should you do?

Stop what you're doing. Assess the situation. Start again with a fresh approach.

After you've stopped your current efforts, I'd advise that you sit down and make a list of all the steps you took in your first effort to be successful with social media. Were there missing elements? Did you see some bottlenecks in your processes? Did you review other social media accounts in your industry to see how you compared? Did you fail to post regularly or follow up on responses from clients, or post at bad times? There are many factors to consider when assessing your success and failure. Perhaps what you think of as failure is actually the next step on the road to accomplishing your goals.

We'll cover many tips and steps I'd like for you to consider later in the book, but for now please take this opportunity to assess how things went honestly. It may well be that after you've carefully considered the project, you'll find some simple corrections you could make that would result in things working out much better.

Let me share a few thoughts that come to mind from previous hard-won experience by myself and others I've worked with in this industry.

First off, not having a good plan in place is a recipe for disaster. If you've decided to dive in, that's noble and brave on the one hand, impractical on the other. You can certainly connect with people online that way, but you may not be making the right connections. It's essential to research and lay out a strategy before you ever sign up for a social media platform.

Think of it as a business proposition. It's true that social media will not usually directly result in a lot of one-on-one sales. You don't put up a virtual storefront through Twitter, for instance. It's the connections to networks – think of them as new markets to explore for your business – that result in sales. Those sales directly linked to your social media campaigns may be better in the long run if you can quantify how often your posts are resulting in a successful call-to-action, rather than taking sales at face value. So be sure you lay out the risks, resources needed, and justification before you proceed. By the way, reading this book counts as research.

After you'd developed your initial strategy, did you put in place a disciplined approach to monitoring your operations? If you took a hit-and-miss approach, it's not likely you'll have a lot of success. Any success you did count wasn't built up to help you advance to the next stage of your efforts.

A social media project needs to be analysed while it's in progress. Did you ever examine any of the metrics: the leading indicators of your message's reach and engagement? It's not enough to do a simple headcount of followers and fans in this era, and no social media expert measures their success solely by those numbers. You need to be tracking engagement and click-throughs as well, for instance.

The problem with metrics – and we'll dive into those more deeply when we talk about analysis and review – is that they can be misleading if you don't know what you're looking for. If you're measuring success by the wrong factors, you may be mistaken in your assessment. It's possible you just have a few small steps to overcome before moving on to the next big phase in your social media presence.

After you've assessed and figured out the things that worked and didn't work, have you considered the fact it may be easier than you think to start over? You already have your previous experience to build from. If you could go back in time and change anything, what would you change? In a way, you get to do that with social media. Because it's very much an "of the moment" technology, your previous mistakes won't be held against you for any length of time. What matters is what you're doing right now and how you plan to handle your business in the future.

As an example, let's say you developed a blog, but you had very little readership and engagement. If you found that the first time you blogged you were reluctant to answer comments, consider responding. If you found your blog wasn't getting a lot of clicks, think about where you're linking the blog. Were your topics not of much interest to those people who were following you? Don't be afraid to ask what they want to hear. Did you run out of things to talk about? Perhaps you should reach out to guest bloggers. Did you tend to post irregularly? Then set up a schedule and let your followers know the expectations for posts. There are a lot of little ways to change things up, and perhaps a rebranding and relaunch is the way to go to enthuse your remaining audience and add new readers into the fold.

I understand that you've put a lot of effort into this already and you may feel the best thing you can do is toss everything out and walk away from it. Cutting ties is much easier than facing missteps and correcting them. Avoid that temptation! Instead, learn from the mistakes you've made, implement a better plan for success, and find the things that are working that you're not aware of.

Even after you've reviewed all the issues that didn't work out, your next worry might be much simpler. Why even bother? How does social media help you build your business?

Chapter 8

Not Convinced Of The Benefits

"It's all so new and I doubt all these social media experts know what they're really doing yet. How do I know any of this effort into social media is going to translate into greater sales?"

I suspect you already think there may be some benefits to social media, or you wouldn't have gotten this far into the book. Let's talk about them.

On a personal level, social media can help keep you informed and current. It can augment your training and connect you with peers, along with helping keep you in better touch with friends and family who are already using these platforms. Of course, just like all offerings found online, you'll want to take anything you find on social media with a grain of salt. Check sources for everything. I'll talk more about that later.

By far the biggest value will be to your brand. If you're serious about improving your personal public profile or growing your business, then you need to be on social media. If you're involved in a non-profit, pledges of support are still a part of your organisation's requirements. Whether you're interested in recruiting, outreach, sales, or developing brand loyalty, it's undeniable that you'll find benefit through social media.

As we've discussed, these social media platforms are new outlets for getting your information out there. They're also a fresh way to interact with people you'd never have connected with before. They may stumble across you through a friend. You may be recommended to them by a positive interaction with other clients. All it takes is a single mention of you by a follower to their followers and fans.

Apart from increasing your brand's visibility, you can also improve your loyalty with those who are already into your message. According to Convince & Convert Digital Marketing Advisors[2], a study showed Americans following their favourite brands on social media become more loyal to them.

Loyalty to companies is particularly strong with the younger set: 66% of 18–24-year-old Americans following a company are more loyal to that companies. Among 25–34-year-olds it's 60%; 53% among 35–44 year olds; 45% among 45–54 year olds; and finally 39% among the 55 and older social media users.

While those numbers may suggest mature professionals aren't interested in your company being on social media, that's not necessarily true. We're only less encouraged than younger users, but 39–53% among 35 and older users is nothing to scoff at.

Returning to print and traditional advertising, consider the advertising you may have already paid for this year. Whether it's television, Internet, radio, or print, you are paying for specific demographics to have access to your advertising. Social media is

[2]   Baer, Jay, "53% Of Americans Who Follow Brands In Social Are More Loyal To Those Brands", Convince & Convert Digital Marketing Advisors, LLC, 2012. Web, 30 May, 2015

special in that your name can appear in a positive way through your fans. Assuming you're not the subject of a negative social media engagement, you've got people's friends – a very trusted community indeed – supporting your product. This is the kind of place you want to be as an advertiser. Following on from that trusted community, you can use social media ambassadors such as your employees to advocate your brand or company. Another name for it is *Employee Advocacy Program*.

Are you still trying to get people to your website? Need them to buy online? Your social media program is perfect for keeping costs down and improving the amount of traffic to your site. By linking your site through social media, it's entirely possible to draw in more clicks, presuming that your content is up to the task.

Speaking of content, consider making sure that your information is ready for the modern world. If you have a website that's not mobile compatible, you're missing a world of potential sales. Make sure that all of your web material is readable via mobile. The Pew Research Center indicated that as of October 2014, 64% of Americans owned a smartphone, while in January 2014 90% owned a cell phone, 32% owned an e-reader, and 42% owned a tablet computer.[3]

Meanwhile, the Australian Bureau of Statistics shows that there were more mobile and fixed wireless users (47.8%) than there were DSL subscribers (40.2%) by December 2014. Going back to June 2006, mobile only accounted for 1.7% of access, while DSL was around the same number. Meanwhile, dial-up

---

[3]   Mobile Technology Fact Sheet, Pew Research Center, Web, 6 June 2015

(remember dial-up?) was at over 45% in 2006, and is now down to 1.3% by December 2014.[4] You may safely expect that apart from websites, those users are also accessing their Facebook and Twitter accounts. The world is getting its information anywhere, any time.

If you're still thinking in dial-up mode, you're seeing the world from ten years ago. And you're missing out.

Social media is an inexpensive entry point to new markets for your brand, considering that the platforms themselves are absolutely free. Advertising on social media platforms such as Facebook isn't that expensive, either. In the old print days, you may have been used to paying by the word in classified advertising in newspapers. If you could afford it, you'd move up to magazines, then radio, and finally television advertising. As of March 2015, Facebook had 1.415 billion users according to the statistics portal Statista.[5] That's a lot more eyeballs than your local newspaper could offer.

That's just the leading platform. Facebook Messenger, the built-in chat system for Facebook, weighs in at 500 million users. LinkedIn is at 347, Google+ and Instagram at 300 million each, Twitter has 288 million, and Tumblr 230 million.

With those numbers behind them, it's clear the world expects to reach you and be reached by you online, both at home and on

---

[4]   Internet Activity, Australia, December 2014, Australian Bureau of Statistics, 1 April 2015. Web, 6 June 2015.

[5]   Leading social networks worldwide as of March 2015, ranked by number of active users (in millions), Statista, March 2015. Web, 6 June 2015.

their phones. It's time to take social media seriously. Don't wait a moment longer.

Of course, another fear that might be holding you back is one we all experience from time-to-time: a very human fear of making mistakes.

Chapter 9

Worry About Making Mistakes

"I'm not about to become one of those execs who blasts out a message to the entire company or all our clients and later on gets pilloried over a typo. I could really screw this up. Even if I delegate and stay out of the social media thing myself, what if my team messes up? The stakes are just too high."

I'm sure you've heard the negative stories of celebrities, politicians, and companies finding themselves on the wrong end of a social media gaffe. The power of social media is such that unforced errors can, indeed, quickly become magnified. Consequently it can seem like the technology could have terrible impacts on a business's reputation. This is an understandable concern.

It may help to keep in mind that we all make unintentional communications mistakes all the time without even realising it. While the best professional communicators take every precaution to try to write or speak with their target audience in mind, it's not possible to know precisely what that audience is thinking as they take in what you have to say. Everything we communicate, including the words you're reading on this page, is going to be filtered and interpreted by individuals in unpredictable ways. They'll relate to your intentions through the lens of their own experiences. This is why it's a best practice to reach the majority of your audience by writing and speaking in plain language, identifying their interests and reasons for communicating, and building your audience's trust over time.

Social media's power as a message distributor has made the speed with which people respond to our missteps faster than ever, and that is undeniably worrying for many people our age. Yet that same medium has an underlying structural ability to help us absorb and learn from our mistakes. Savvy users in our audience already know this, because they too have taken their share of missteps. Furthermore, if you plan accordingly for the inevitability of errors, those horror stories you've heard about can be avoided, or at least handled in such a way as to recover audience goodwill.

Social media *is* a new development within the communications landscape, and we're all learning. It may not be as uncharted as it was when Friendster first emerged in 2002, but because of the ever-changing platforms and models being used, communicators are learning to stay on top of these new developments. Consequently, mistakes happen.

As we consider the lessons learned from our mistakes and from others, we can discover there's really nothing to fear at all.

You may fear that anything you put out there, in particular little things like spelling errors, broken links, and minor gaffes, is likely to harm your organisation and your reputation. There's no question that you want to release the most professional materials you can every time you hit send, just as you would for any other medium. It's not a great idea to post anything and everything that comes to your mind on the spur of the moment, just as you shouldn't fire off an email without running it through spell-check or be less than fully prepared when meeting with a new client.

However, the nature of social media is incredibly forgiving towards the bulk of common mistakes people make. If you make a simple mistake, the odds favour your error having a very short lifespan. Tweets, as one example, have a ridiculously short half-life. As noted by the blog Wisemetrics in their article "Your Tweet Half-life Is 1 Billion Times Shorter Than Carbon-14's", that half-life, or median engagement over time for a tweet, has been subject to several different measurements. Some sources put the half-life at between five minutes and 2.8 hours, while Wisemetrics calculates its median engagement time to be 24 minutes.[6] They go a step further and note that their research indicates a Facebook post's half-life is 90 minutes.

Just like an error posted on a webpage, you should feel free to go back and issue corrections. If the mistake is minor and has had relatively little engagement, get rid of the offending tweet or post and replace it with an appropriate one. Social media is archived and no mistake is ever truly removed. However, for minor issues the audience's memory and interest in a small mistake is minimal.

If the mistake is larger or too many people have seen it and commented on it, rather than scrubbing the post, consider issuing a clarification. Just as you might for a widely-distributed press release with a factual error, you can set the record straight. Let people know you care about the consequences of what you say

6 Rey, Benjamin, "Your Tweet Half-life Is 1 Billion Times Shorter Than Carbon-14's", Wisemetrics, 5 March 2014. Web, 23 May 2015.

and that you're paying attention. We're all human. Showing a little humility by making the fix says you care about your reputation, and people will think better of you for it.

While the short half-life of communications means the vast majority of mistakes you might make could end up being overlooked, there's another aspect to the rapid back-and-forth nature of social media to consider. Whether it's 24 minutes or 2.8 hours, that's a very short window of time for engaging with your audience. If you wish to have any sort of impact at all and grow your audience, frequent engagement through posts, videos, and images is essential to success. Bear in mind, social media is also self-selecting. No one's going to follow you who doesn't want to. Your audience wants those messages, so it's okay to talk with them regularly and often.

With any relationship, there's always the danger of miscommunication. The strength of that relationship and its reputation is built on regular conversation. It depends on you speaking your intentions as clearly as possible, listening to what the others involved in the conversation have to say, and responding appropriately when called upon. Over time, relationships and brands develop trust through this natural process.

When mistakes arise in any communications – and they will – it will be the trust you've built through long-term engagement that'll help carry you through. This core communications concept carries over quite well from the era of print to digital mediums – better in some ways. With social media there's an actual conversation being held, as opposed to the one-way press releases of old.

Additionally and importantly, there are steps you can take to plan for an appropriate response and recover from the error gracefully. We'll look at the five step process for appropriate social media planning later on in Section 3.

First, we have another concern to address – the worry that you don't even need social media for your business.

Chapter 10

Don't Believe That Your Business Needs Social Media

"I can see how social media is going to benefit folks whose core business involves interacting with the public. We don't have much of that going on. I think we can take a pass on this."

As I've already amply illustrated, social media is deeply enmeshed within the global market. However, you may belong to that very limited class of professionals who don't see a place for themselves and what they do in the social media world. If so, I have a surprise for you.

You're missing out.

Does your business consist of one person interacting solely with one person – you? If that's the case, you have no need for social media. For every other business, you have little choice. You are expected to engage. And I should hasten to add, that first business is pure fiction. We live in a world of people and no worker is an island.

Trust me – no matter what line of work you're in, you'll have like-minded industry professionals you can connect with to help you stay up on what's most current in industry trends. You can't afford to pass up on any opportunity to stay in touch. But if that were the only reason you were likely to get into social media, I can understand why you'd be hesitant. So let's focus instead on discussing professionals who seem, at face value, to be in more isolated lines of work.

Consider professionals like myself – writers. If an author is writing a book, you may consider that a fairly isolated business model. As I sit here with my headphones on, typing away, I can certainly see why you'd think that. The only interactions an author might have on a regular basis would be with their literary agent, editors, and publisher.

One problem with that, of course – that's no longer the business model at all! So allow me to use my own business as a model for why yours has changed in ways you may not even realise.

The online self-publishing revolution has shaken the print industry, allowing writers with large followings and dedicated readers the capacity to deal directly with their buyers. While they may still need to attend book signings and pay for traditional print advertising, more and more they are required to maintain active websites, blogs, and social media accounts. The digital interaction can be quite interesting: the writer may have a new book coming out and wants to let people know about it. They're going to upload the finished work, write a blog post about the book, direct buyers to the site where they can buy the book, and alert their social media communities about the new product through a post containing a link. The process, excluding the book upload, may be repeated a number of times, depending on the particular platform.

You'd think that's all there is to the process. It's not. Authors are finding fellow critique experts and editors online, and they may very well find them through Twitter or Facebook. They're connecting with their fellow writers and with literary agents online, and that includes through social media. There are contests taking place online through Twitter in which writers write their 140 character pitches, hoping that agents like their ideas. If they do, that'll mean they want to see more.

Once the connection with the agents is made, the process usually continues electronically. The days of laboriously printing out a paper manuscript and firing it off to literary agents via mail are over. Most agents prefer email submissions; rounds of drafts and revisions take place electronically.

Perhaps your business doesn't deal with a lot of direct customers through sales. Let's consider a non-profit charitable organisation. You may think that these organisations' communications would primarily be one-directional. They send out a request for aid and support, then the recipient sends in funds.

However, hosting a website and sending out flyers costs money. With zero entry fee for social media platform use, you have a wonderful opportunity to connect regularly with donors and receive input. Those connections may result in great suggestions and input into how to target your spending on projects donors truly connect with. If you have a project that needs more explanation, this is the best possible way to get the message out there.

Another business model might be the more industrial concerns who have almost no dealings with the public. Their only interactions come in the form of basic press releases, and if we're honest, most of those are sent to trade organisations rather than communities. These are businesses that don't necessarily see a need for a big social media communications push.

However, I promise you that you still need to engage with the public to some extent. If there are concerns about your industry, you have no better opportunity to educate and engage the public than with social media. After all, no matter what industry you're in, you're ultimately doing work that's intended to benefit society in some way.

If you encounter a situation in which you need to inform the public about why you're doing something, you have a ready means of reaching them. By being an active member of your community, you can have a better impact on people who are influential both in the network and in letting people know your side of the story.

Of course, every business has employees. Yes, there are many ways of reaching employees that don't involve social media, yet if you had a means of hiring and drawing the best possible talent to work for your company without spending a lot of money, wouldn't you want to try it? Posting job positions on LinkedIn, Facebook, Twitter, Google+, and possibly even Tumblr will help get your message out there and connect you with your future workforce.

Letting people know that you're advertising a position on social media also speaks of you being relevant and your company keeping up with the latest trends. If people expect to hear from you on social media via messaging, you can use this opportunity to highlight your recruitment effort. Link to recruitment videos on video-sharing platforms, share insights into what it's like to work for your company via blogs, and let people see some of the folks they'll be working with through photos. It's a great opportunity to connect with the next generation of employees.

Now that we've overcome most of your concerns, let's talk about the last big one on the list: a fear of appearing to be overly self-involved.

Chapter 11

Appearing Narcissistic

"I want people to focus on our mission, not our personalities. I don't need people to think I've got an overinflated ego. This just isn't right for me and could, potentially, really backfire and make everyone think I'm an egomaniac."

This is a common concern for folks who are modest or who are worried about how they will come off on social media. Like all of the concerns I've noted, I can see why you would be worried about this. But I promise you, it's going to be just fine.

Simply having a social media presence does *not* make you narcissistic, and no one you interact with will think that of you. If you aren't a narcissist when you lead meetings, conduct workshops, or address the press, you aren't a narcissist in this context either. Social media is no more than a network, no different from the many networks you involve yourself in during your real life.

Networks are an essential part of your work life and your personal life. If you extend the same courtesies to others online that you do in person, you're not a narcissist.

If you are involved in weekend and evening activities, you know there's a time and place to speak and be heard. Sharing your thoughts as a mature professional is something that is sought after.

Still not convinced? Don't worry. Your audience will let you know if they think you're too self-involved. They'll simply stop listening and cut you out of their social media news feeds. You'll see it when you look at how many followers and fans you stay connected to.

Besides, have you thought about everyone you're already speaking to? They're also on social media holding conversations, talking about their experiences, and sharing their ideas with your networks. It would be strange if they all suddenly turned on you, yelled "Narcissist", and then went right back to tweeting about the person who cut them up in traffic.

But in all seriousness, if you're the kind of person who regularly listens as well as speaks, who seeks to build up and support friendships, and who stays in touch regularly with your connections, you're already a natural for social media. Everyone else is involved in the same process of information sharing. This is where you belong, and you have strengths to share with many communities.

You may, at this point, feel like the over-sharing culture that's sprung up from social media has become a negative facet of society. If you see younger people on smartphones typing away and feel like they've disconnected themselves from society, you're not alone in that observation. It's definitely important to have genuine conversations with actual people in the room.

Whenever I find myself checking up on statuses in a public setting, I make a conscious effort to put my phone away and be ready to talk to those around me, if they're so inclined. I like to think it's no different from a time when people used to read newspapers and books more frequently in public. If one has the opportunity to engage face to face with people, put the phone and the newspaper down. If the time is right, be social in real life. Talk to real people.

At the same time, bear in mind that this virtual coffee shop is where a lot of the action can be found, particularly when it comes to professional development. It's not entirely bad. Consider all the people in the world with limited mobility or access to people outside of their own immediate family and friends. Social media has given millions of people access to communities and knowledge they'd never otherwise have connected with. It's the most powerful networking tool imaginable, and for your professional development, it's totally fine to join in and share your thoughts.

Social media's name makes it clear: you're meant to be social, not talk to hear your own voice. When you put a message out into the world, it's on you to make sure people want to hear what you have to say. If you can do that, you have nothing at all to be worried about.

When you're conversing on social media, it's a simple matter to avoid seeming too self-important. We'll cover some golden rules of conversation later on in the book, but in the meantime just remember a few major points. Focus on what others are saying, give generously when asked your opinion, and share when others have something they want to communicate. Don't be shy and don't dominate conversations. Be sharing, be topical, be caring, and you can't go wrong.

If you're mentoring others, you're not self-absorbed. Immerse yourself in the conversations and you'll be fine.

Don't forget that in your role as an experienced professional, you're also representing your organisation in the things you do. If you want your organisation to have a voice in the places where it counts, you absolutely must demonstrate some personal leadership. Be sure you're putting your best foot forward and talking about the things that matter to people in your communities.

Have we overcome all of your fears? I certainly hope so. There's no way in a book of this scope to cover everything, but I hope you are adventurous enough to reconsider your worries and be willing to tackle new things. And so we come to the constructive part of the book, in which we find the five steps that lead to success.

Section 3

The Five Step Process

I've tried to review comprehensively why you've put off engaging in social storytelling. If you're ready to set aside your fears, there are five steps we can follow to help you get the most benefit from your new collection of platforms and communities.

Chapter 12

Understand The Customer (That Can Also Mean You)

Yes, you read that right. When it comes to social media, you can be the customer as well. As an engaged member of a social media community, you should have a reasonable expectation of personally benefiting from your online experiences. I want to talk about some of those benefits first, then discuss what your customer is looking for from you.

You As The Customer

Before you read this book, you'd either decided to opt out of social media or you hadn't made up your mind. If you're reconsidering, now is the time to think about what you'll be getting out of all of this. What are your goals? I'll offer you a few that you should consider, but ultimately you'll still need to determine what's most important for you and your business.

You may be participating in social media to take part in industry conversations with your peers. It may be that you're looking to connect with partners for your business. You may wish to poll your community to help you decide on some aspect of your business, from a potential renaming to a new product. Naturally, you may need to increase the number of clients you work with or the customers whom you sell to. However you wish to approach this process, understand that you're getting something from it as well.

So long as you're clear on what you want, you're in a better position to look into what other members of your business network are looking for from you.

Research Your Own Customers

One of the first steps in this process I'd suggest you do is to review a large number of competing or partner organisations in your industry. See what they already have out there in terms of social media. Get to know their platforms, their monitoring and interaction practices, and the content they're putting out there.

When you review the other social media actors, ask yourself a few questions. What sort of engagements are you seeing? If you see a competitor with a Facebook page full of complaints and no responses, that's certainly a nice model for you to avoid. Does your business partner have a social media presence in which they're constantly arguing with their community? Also not the best model to follow.

Take note of the things you see out there, both those that are working and those that aren't. Pay special attention to customer exchanges. If you see a high proportion of complaints being respectfully, quickly, and successfully turned from negative to positive experiences, think about the procedures you could put in place to emulate that model.

Apart from the exchanges, see how visitors are responding to the messaging that's being targeted at them.

Once you have a good understanding of the terrain, take things a step further. Social media allows you to see what people think of you and your competitors through searches. Feel free to search through the social media tools available online to see what people are saying about your competitors, partners, and you. This should be the very first step in what will eventually become a robust listening program. Remember: social media requires listening in the same proportion as you're talking. If you're simply chatting up the room and not hearing what others are saying, you'll quickly be identified as insincere and will be dismissed.

Asking Your Audience

What else can you do to get to know your audience? Try asking them! Many social media platforms offer a polling option where you can ask your questions. If you don't want to be that formal about it, you can simply ask questions and keep an eye on the comments for responses. People do like to be asked questions, in particular if they're being asked their opinion or to share something personal that might make them look good. Regardless of how you approach the questions, don't be afraid to ask.

There are numerous excellent survey tools out there that you can use, some with trial period uses, others requiring a monthly fee. Be sure to check around for the tool that's going to work best for you.

You can also find both persona and data tools that give you a good idea of how you're already being seen if you have an existing social media presence. These tools will be most helpful in moving on to your second or later generation social media platforms.

Getting To Know Your Audience Through Platforms

When you're thinking about the audience you need to speak with, consider each individual platform based on the folks who are actually using it. Let's take a look here at the differences.

Each social media platform has a different demographic that it tends to appeal to. You can easily research each platform in advance to see if it works for you. For instance, Pinterest is quite popular with women. Tumblr is most closely associated with younger users. However, it's also important to know that you have material that suits each demographic's needs. If you don't have any images to share, you have nothing much worth sharing on Pinterest. This may be an area you want to develop more through photography. An argument in favour of doing so: you can reach audiences on popular social media platforms such as Instagram, Pinterest, and Flickr. Other platforms such as Google+, Facebook, Twitter, and Tumblr are growing friendlier with images as well.

The same can be said for Vine and YouTube video postings. Videos are easy to create using technology as basic as a phone, though you may want to invest in video editing software. If you do create videos, know your audience. Videos that run over three minutes are usually considered too long. The sweet spot should be more like one and a half to two minutes. Don't forget to do a careful job with close captioning your video. It's important to be accessible to all your clients, including the hearing-impaired. While YouTube can automatically generate captions, it's a good practice to review the captions and update them as necessary. It's not a difficult task (though potentially time-consuming, if you decided to make your video much more than two minutes), so feel free to delegate that to someone.

Both images and videos enhance your presence on all social media platforms. They provide a nice graphic punctuation to your text-based conversations with your audience. Even if it's just creating a short graphic with a quote or text on it, this will have a better impact on your audience's response.

When it comes to quality, remember that production value is important. Social media may be quick and inexpensive, but those consuming it still expect the best possible effort on your part to be entertaining and informative.

What About Internal Audiences?

Before you launch an internal social media platform, you can ask your employees what they're interested in talking about. It'll help ease their transition into the cultural change that's coming. When you're checking the employee expectations for social media, find out if there are any specific internal issues that need to be communicated.

If your employees are struggling to manage their documents, to share their information with the right department, and can't keep up with a massive amount of email that they have coming in, this could be the solution. See if there are additional issues within the organisation that social media can solve.

Target That Message

Once you've got an idea of what your audience expects from you, it can be much easier to target future messaging. Whether it's walking your customers through every step of the purchase or getting feedback on the latest innovation your organisation has released, you'll know what they're looking for.

When you have your audience in mind, write for them. Then you should plan to purchase advertising, as needed and budgeted, for that particular audience. Most advertising plans on social media consider all of the potential demographics that you'll be able to research later though metrics. Once your social media is up and running, you'll be able to confirm your early assumptions regarding your audience through metrics analysis.

The interesting thing about social media audiences is that you never know who will actually be listening in. Remember that social media has the capability of being free, paid, and shared. Your audience will come from all corners, so don't be surprised if the actual results turn out to be quite different from your initial research. That's okay, so long as you're reaching the customers you need to reach. If your audience isn't what you expected, craft a message and campaign that's designed to target your desired audience.

Now you've done the legwork and are ready to go. You know who you're talking to and what you want to get out of this effort. Let's start thinking about planning and strategy.

Chapter 13

Planning And Strategy

Now let's discuss the things you should do prior to signing on to a single social media platform for professional reasons.

You're ready to dive right in? Good! I'm sure you're deeply experienced in business plans and proposals. Before you take another step, sit down with the people you think you'll be most involved in this process with and agree to develop a social media proposal. In doing so, you need to consider everything we've covered in Chapter 12. Your audience will help you determine the first things to do for your planning.

Set Your Goals

If you're about to sign on to a platform, consider what you want to call your goal. What are you trying to accomplish through social media? Are there multiple goals? Are some of those goals a higher priority than others? Developing a clear mission for your platform will help you keep on task. As you develop your goals, be sure your objectives throughout the plan make sense and are ready to be executed.

Design a mission that works for you and your organisation. For instance, if you develop an Instagram account, you should want to share images for a very specific reason. The mission might in some way connect to sales, developing your brand, or improving your professional standing. Whatever that mission may be, put the mission in words and on paper, not just in your head. Then plan to follow through with that mission.

If you've mastered the bulk of this by making sure you understand your goals, your employees' goals, and your customers' and partners' goals, you should be ready to proceed.

Work With Professionals

At this stage of development, if you were to have a professional working with you who'd be responsible for helping you with this level of planning, they would likely be your social media strategist. The strategist can help you navigate the bewildering world of social media platforms by helping you determine which would be a good fit for your brand and how to make them work for you.

By the way, there are a number of titles out there within the social media profession, and they can be confusing. They are by no means universal. However, the strategist is the person who, by and large, does what their title sounds like. In addition to the initial and ongoing strategy development, they're likely to be essential to planning which platforms you'll engage more in over others, which new platforms you'll take on, and which ones you'll cut loose if it becomes necessary. They may also help you to design and implement specific aspects of campaigns, lay out a calendar for future communications on the platforms, and manage any community managers below them.

You're going to need more than just a social media expert, though. Have your marketing, legal, and HR teams on board for this effort. Marketing's purpose should be fairly obvious, as we've mentioned the need to work with them for building your brand identity. Legal will be necessary in helping you define your social media policies and responses. HR will help you with the hiring end of things, in particular in making sure you have skilled social media members on board.

When you have your professionals in place to help you with the process, it's time to figure out how this fits into your overall communications plan.

Fitting Social Media In With Your Communications Plan

You may reasonably consider how this new program should fit in with the rest of your communications efforts, both digital and print. For the most part, they all remain relevant. If you've been finding that your company is moving away from print and towards digital, social media isn't going to alter that equation one way or the other. It's probably most helpful to think of social media as being less about finding a distribution chain and more about connecting with communities interested in what you have to say.

Essentially, you're still going to want to provide information through email, mailings, websites – all the ways the public used to come to you for information – but you may find you're investing less time and money into some of these. When you figure out what the balance should be, plan accordingly. In the meantime, you'll be planning to reach all of those audiences who expect you to come to them.

Communications Planning

Just as you should have a crisis communications plan in place for your normal communications processes, it's important to be prepared to deal with controversy in social media. The nature of social media is that anyone and everyone can theoretically reach your presence and converse with you. You may not like what you hear. Are you ready to respond? Be ready!

There are a few ways to handle these conversations. One way would be, of course, to block the messengers, delete the messages, and refuse to speak. Can I give you a word of advice here? This is a terrible solution.

By all means, plan to block and delete posts from users who are clearly spamming you (that is, not communicating with you but using your platform for their own purposes, usually sales or clicks). You should feel free to do the same to users who are racist or abusive. I would suggest that it's a great idea to have a written policy on how you handle such posts, and make that policy clear and readable for your users. You can share that through the information section of the social media platform – virtually every platform has a section where you add outside links, and it's an excellent way to connect users to this knowledge.

Deleting negative comments and blocking users simply for having a negative opinion comes off as heavy-handed. It's much more likely to inspire a legion of negative postings that follow from others. It's also contrary to the concept of having open, honest conversations.

What if there's a conversation taking place through comments and that conversation is negative? Before you're tempted to jump in – in fact, *especially* before you jump in – wait a bit. You may be surprised at what happens. Conversations like this, in particular those that are controversial, can result in people taking your side. While you don't want to encourage a flame war, it's entirely possible that your fans and followers will say exactly the things you would have said anyway. It comes off better when you aren't being defensive and allow the conversation to handle naturally.

When you do weigh in, and you may well need to, it's usually best to provide an authoritative statement that explains your organisation's stance on a topic. This may not change minds, in particular those of activists who are strongly opposed to what you do. However, it's still important to share your official stance for those who haven't got a stake in the argument. Make your position clear once, and let that be enough. There's no need to correct everyone who has a difference of opinion; it's often counterproductive and rarely leaves you in a positive light.

Shortening Your URLs

It's a minor item, but as we haven't addressed it I want to mention it now. Have a plan in order to shorten URLs for social media. It's not an essential factor for most of your platforms, but with Twitter you absolutely need the shortened URLs to fit everything within 140 characters.

The nice thing about these shortened URLs, regardless of where you use them, is that you can possibly receive some extra metrics and information through the URL shortener.

So now you know what your audience wants, what they like, what they're like, and how to deal with the bad eggs in the bunch, what next? Great question. It's time to set up and design the actual platforms and systems you'll put in place to make your communications efforts work for you.

One At A Time, A Little At A Time

It may be tempting to develop all of your social media platforms at once. I'd encourage you to hold off on that. When it comes to launching, it's always best to start off slow and build yourself up a bit at a time.

Start off with a single platform and, if this is your first platform, soft launch it. When I say soft launch, I mean you needn't be overly aggressive in letting people know your creation exists – at first. Post a few items, provide a small announcement somewhere to let people know you've launched, but don't put the word out to everyone you know just yet. Allow your platform to grow a little over a few weeks to make sure everything is up and running smoothly.

After you've committed to creating an account, monitor it and work with it for that soft launch. If everything is going well, go ahead and let everyone know about your platform. You can then consider launching a second platform a month or two after your initial platform is on the ground and running.

Chapter 14

Setup And Design

If you're all ready to get started and have a great plan in order, the thing to do is begin to put together your social media presence. On the surface, that may seem like it's little more than signing up for a service and posting your "Hello, world" announcement.

Social media is simple to use on a daily basis. The advance setup is also simple, intentionally so. There's not much to creating an account and posting on it, if you take the scattershot method.

That's fine for your personal non-branded social media. However, there are a number of important steps to consider when laying out your project for professional and organisational reasons. They are accounts management, community management, look and feel, information workflow, communications policies, operations, crafting starting messages, crosslinking, getting the word out.

Sounds like a lot? It's not so bad. We'll take them each one step at a time.

Accounts Management

If you're planning to develop a company-wide internal and/or external social media presence, you're going to need to appoint someone to hold the keys. That may be more than one somebody, but whomever is charged with this task will have a few duties that come with the job. This is where your social media manager (whether internal or outsourced) comes into play.

This is the person who's essentially in charge of taking care of the internal workings of the account. They may "own" the account or they may be delegated to own it for you. They're charged with making the platform work for your organisation, in particular when you need changes made that aren't just creating new posts.

One crucial aspect of accounts management is to change passwords consistently and regularly. If you use the same password for every social media platform and if they are easy to guess, you are putting yourself and your organisation at risk of being hacked.

Although there are websites with random password generators and management available such as Last Pass or 1Password, a sentence with spaces in it including capital letters, numbers, and characters can be quite effective.

Example: DON'T 5 underbake – supp0rt?

The account holder will probably be responsible for implementing any changes to images such as banners and logos. They may be charged with adding new administrators and implementing any setting changes. They may or may not be required to monitor and update posts, but this is an administrative requirement that may be shared – it may be that they never craft a single message for this account. It's up to you how you choose to delegate these tasks.

Community Management

Decide who you're going to have manage your internal and external communications. If you're only creating a personal presence, this can be simplified by being prepared to listen and respond, but if you find you can't handle the amount of incoming traffic, it may be necessary to delegate in part. However, if the account is geared towards advancing your personal brand – that is, if this is less an organisational account and more of a personally-branded account – anything that you say really should be coming from you when possible. It's preferable to going through a writer on your staff speaking as you. Stand by your own words and be genuine, and the communities you involve yourself in will appreciate it.

For an internal and external non-personal social media presence, a community manager can help keep your discussions on track and relevant.

Look And Feel

Most social media platforms allow a degree of customisation. Whether it's the background image, the banner, or the information you provide to your customers, you'll need to review all of the settings and set appropriate graphics and images for that platform. Be sure to adhere to the platform's image size requirements and be mindful of any buttons or widgets that may inadvertently block your full message.

I'd also encourage you to bring your website architect into this discussion. If you've established a specific look and feel for your website, you could, and perhaps should, extend that branding to your social media platforms.

Information Workflow

As you may already do for public enquiries, you'll need to establish a workflow for the answering of queries. When the public contacts you, either directly through the social media platform's inbox or through a more public message, it's your responsibility to respond in a timely fashion. Set that expectation by having an internal information workflow determined in advance of launching your social media presence.

Determine who will monitor and review incoming communications, who your subject matter experts are, and who will craft the response to those enquiring. When everyone is clear regarding their roles, it should be a simple matter of directing the workflow and seeing the results. You may wish to aim for a 24 hour or faster response time whenever possible to keep up with the flow of information, but above all be accurate. Users will forgive a slower response if their enquiry requires a more thorough investigation.

Communications Policies

Once you have the information workflow sorted out, be prepared to have a discussion with your writers regarding how to post and share information. They may already have training and experience in this area. If so, great! If not, you may still want to have that conversation.

As previously discussed, the platforms have different posting requirements. Experiment before launching your social media presence on a platform if you're unsure how they work.

For instance, as of May 2015, posting a link on Facebook will create an auto-generated preview of the title for the link, a little descriptive text, and possibly an accompanying image. You can scroll through the potential images and replace it with a better one. You can also retitle the link and change the accompanying text.

Sounds like a lot to know? Each platform is different and has its own peculiarities. For that reason, it's great to check them out in advance.

Once you're comfortable, make sure everyone on the communications team is on board. That may include making sure they'll monitor hashtags, video settings, image settings, and the amount of text that will be visible to posters.

Operations

Just as you need to have an information workflow, you have to have a plan to monitor and engage with your audience regularly through your platforms. This may include some of the following operational needs:

- Watching for updates to the platform
- Updating the passwords on a regular basis
- Responding to enquiries
- Planning for regular communications
- Measuring the metrics that help you determine your level of success.

While we've considered some of these individual requirements earlier in this chapter, it may be useful to take a holistic approach in planning these responsibilities. If you're considering establishing a one-person team, now is the time to set that in stone. If you're the one-person team, it's good to know everything you're up against. But operations imply regular ongoing maintenance. Here's where you decide all the components of making that work.

If you're already managing a website or a communications team, much of this won't be all that new. Website designs and technology constantly shift and change, requiring regular training. So too do social media platforms: third-party configurations that users must be prepared to adjust to.

When you've determined who will be responsible for which roles, you are well on your way to having the setup and design adequately planned for.

Craft Starting Messages

The social media platforms you'll be working with always feature the option of holding back before going "live"; that is, not allowing the general public to see the site before it's ready. You don't want to go live without any sort of messaging whatsoever, so I recommend creating one or two early posts, images, and videos (as appropriate) that already exist on the site beforehand. This is going to be better than an empty site for most of your platforms. The only exception might be Twitter, which is much more "of the moment" than other social media. You want people to see your tweets as soon as they're ready to go out. On the other hand, there's no point to a YouTube channel or Pinterest board without videos and images. Create content as appropriate in advance.

Crosslinking And Getting The Word Out

As part of your overall marketing plan, it's a good practice to get the word out on the existence of your social media platforms. If you have a website, have you found a way to integrate your social media presence with it? Are there similar organisations that would be willing to let the world know about your presence? Do you have a mailing list? Any of these outlets may be appropriate as a means of getting the word out about your product. Reach out to them and let them know you exist. If you're generous about sharing their material, they may be more inclined to magnify your message.

Don't forget to crosslink and share on your social media platforms as well. If you have a Facebook presence already and are just about to launch your Twitter account, you might mention this on Facebook.

All set? Let's move on to analysis and review.

Chapter 15

Analyse And Review

Once everything in your planning and strategy session is ready to go, it's time to begin the less exciting but entirely necessary process of analysing your social media presence and reviewing your progress. It's not as sexy, but analysis is vital to keeping your program moving forward and successful.

One of the things you should always keep an eye on within the realm of social media is the metrics. Nearly every platform you'll be working with has an internal metrics system built in. Don't worry if one doesn't or if you're unhappy with what you're using. There is a wealth of third party tools available for analysis.

Unfortunately, I can't tell you how to measure your social media success through metrics. Success and the relative measure of value for your organisation will have to be determined through your own set of goals. Remember when we discussed goals in Chapter 13? Continue with that thinking as you develop metrics.

While it's tempting to think of metrics in terms of how many people are visiting your social media, consider that part of your goals should be to create action among those users.

Internal Metrics Systems

Virtually every social media platform has an internal analytics system. Before you take a look, consider these three points:

1. They're not incredibly easy to read or understand the first time you look at them
2. The information they contain may not be applicable to your needs
3. The information they contain may change all the time.

So if you've already clicked one of those buttons and been over-whelmed, take heart! Even social media experts have had the same experience you have had.

Let's talk about what some of those analytics will include and what they mean.

Page views, image views, video views, blog views are essentially what they sound like. That's the raw number of times people have visited your content and accessed the information. What may be of a little more interest is the number of unique visitors for each content area. One person may have looked at the same page seven times, and that would inflate your numbers compared to the number of new visitors who've looked once.

Earlier in the book, we discussed the fact it's possible to mag-nify a post exponentially as people share, comment, and like your post. How many people your post or tweet ultimately *reaches* may be a more useful number to consider, in particular for key messages, than the number of followers and fans you have. Some of those followers may not be that genuine; they may have liked you once, but don't follow your posts very regularly. On certain platforms, they may not even be real. Twitter is well-known for having many accounts that aren't run by real people, but by auto-mated bots. On the other hand, your more dedicated fans may be the ones who are helping get your post magnified, and those fans are quite genuine.

Then the next question you may want to ask is how often people comment, like, or share your information. This is called engagement. When it comes to social media, this is a pretty important consideration. It helps you decide if you're being effective or not in connecting with people.

Reach and engagement are both important, but which is more important to you? It's a tough call. Engagement is always nice, because it shows you that you're interacting with your audience and having the kind of conversations that can lead to action on your audience's part. On the other hand, reach lets you know that you're accessing new audiences and potentially bringing them on as loyal followers and fans.

Some platforms will also tell you important demographic information, including gender and age groups of those visiting. You may be surprised to learn who has an interest in your organisation, but bear in mind that this may be more representative of the population on that platform. Still it's useful to know, in particular when framing your message for that particular audience.

Additionally, you may discover *where* you're most popular. Platform data may include the countries and cities where people like you. Besides the geographic location, you may learn the referrers to your platform or blog. Referrals could be other websites.

It's possible you may receive information about what sort of device people are using to access your social media. Don't be surprised to learn more and more people are accessing social media through their phones.

In addition to the other metrics you can pull together, you may be able to learn how many times your profile has been mentioned over a period of time. Twitter analytics as of June 2015 can do that. They can also tell you the percentage of mentions in comparison to previous times.

A few other things you'll want to keep an eye out for while you're reviewing your metrics are the conversions and leads. Conversions are the number of people who actually did what you wanted them to do, whether it's buying a product or signing up for a newsletter. Leads refer to the people who potentially could become converts. These are things you need to know when trying to sell.

While considering the success, you can also look at the bad things. There's the bounce rate, which tells you the percentage of people who visited and left; the exit rate, which tells you at what point people left; and time on the site, which refers to how long they stuck around before leaving. All of these things give you a better picture of how to improve things.

External Metrics Systems

There are countless third-party social media assessment tools out there, designed to help you get the most out of every platform you have. A few will generate reports, while others can let you know how you match up against other networks in your platform, and possibly within your own region.

These tools are often free for basic information. They offer more detail and in-depth reports for fees. I'm not going to recommend any specifically, as that information can quickly become dated. What works best for me may not work for you. I encourage you to research and try a few tools on your own.

When you have picked an assessment tool, generate a few reports and see if they're providing you with information you can use. If it's not working out, feel free to cancel and try something else.

Putting It All Together

At some point, you may have a superior who will want to know more about how all your hard work is going. Possibly you're the boss, in which case you should have some expectation of receiving reports that make sense. Let's consider what you should be seeing.

Metrics reports are wonderful for the sheer data they provide, but they don't necessarily communicate what you hope to communicate to others. Develop a presentation that tells anyone who looks at it those metrics at a glance.

Before making any assumptions, review the metrics that you've agreed need to be shared. Rather than putting raw numbers into your presentation, clearly state each point of data in a compelling and clear way. For example, you may wish to provide a chart that shows the change in engagement over time. If everyone who will see the report may not be clear on what engagement is, spell it out.

The point of the metrics that you share is to help make decisions. Keep that in mind while you're developing the report.

Audit Your Social Media

When you have a good handle on what you've created, you need to get a handle on your full presence in the social media world. You do this by auditing your social media platforms. You can assign this to your social media strategist if you're not prepared to do this yourself.

Things you should have prepared for your audit:

- Your entire platform listing. Provide the name of the platform and the URLs.
- Search for imposters. Look up your brand name online and identify anything that has been co-opted by people who are posing as you. When you have your list, report them as is possible. Some social media tools such as Twitter allow you to claim your own identity formally for your account.
- Centralise your passwords and make sure they're secured or use a password manager such as Last Pass or 1Password
- Be sure you're well branded across your platforms. This should include all images for banners, profiles, bios, and descriptions.

You can create the audit yourself or search online for an applicable social media audit template that you can download and customise as needed.

Once you've completed your audit, review all of the materials and make sure you're happy with what you see. If you need to make changes, do so now and watch closely to make sure the changes continue to make sense.

The final step of our five step process? Refine and tweak your processes as needed.

Chapter 16
Refine And Tweak

You've decided on your plan of action, have your communication goals in mind, analysed the results, and you're now fully immersed in the world of online communities. Pat yourself on the back, you're all done!

Ah, if only it were that easy, right? Like any serious endeavour, you'll need to continue to refine your efforts and tweak the things that aren't working. These things should, ideally, be a result of your careful attention to the metrics and analysis you developed in the previous chapter. Those results will help point you in the right direction to constant improvement.

When I talked about fears, I mentioned that you'd need to think through your efforts by being flexible. This is the time to do it by implementing the changes you need to make.

Follow Your Own Recommendations

No doubt you've already got a set of ideas you've worked through from the metrics. If engagement is low, this is an area that needs improvement. If reach is consistently low, you may need to improve your outreach messages over your calls to action. Finding the right balance is as much an art as it is a science, so you may have to adjust as needed. However, you should be using the metrics as your roadmap so you are clear on where you're going.

Change Is Good

If something isn't working, change it. If a platform appears to be foundering for some reason, it may be time to think about where people are going for information. In particular, if things are going very badly, consider some of the assessment we discussed back in Chapter 7 about not getting results after a lot of effort. I won't repeat everything I said there, but do recall that you don't simply need to quit your entire work. If you've followed the previous steps of engagement, ideally your efforts won't have gone quite so far off the rails anyway.

Return to the audit that you created and make sure you have a clear listing of all aspects of your social media. Let's say you created a single Twitter account, but you had no intention of creating additional accounts. However, perhaps your organisation has multiple goals. You may need to inform people about your corporate information, hope to recruit new employees, and wish to help customers with their experience. Those three goals may not work out well with a single account after all, so now you should be considering how to divvy up the new accounts and their associated responsibilities.

As you sort that out and make the changes, be sure to work through the first four steps as needed. If you're creating a new platform, you won't have much choice: you'll need to go through all four.

Refine To Meet Goals

Are you still not making sales? It's possible that your plan isn't entirely working in the way you intended. Refine your efforts by checking over your messaging and connections as thoroughly as possible.

It may seem like I've already touched on this thoroughly, but there is slightly more to the picture than meets the eye. Allow me to elaborate.

Let's say you're finding you have a great deal of success with your images and messages posted on Instagram but less so with Pinterest. Why is one community working out for you better than another? That can be hard to say. Checking the metrics may or may not provide the answers.

One possibility is that when you post, your message is resonating better with one community than with another. The thing to do is to experiment and see if slightly different messaging nets you the results you want to see.

I'd also say that if you're going to need to turn off one channel in favour of putting more resources into another, this is the time to do so. Just make sure that you conduct a full "lessons learned" analysis regarding the platform you're walking away from after you've made your decision.

Apart from messages and platforms, are you seeing the desired results from your processes? Are your administrators within your internal social media platform losing interest or not as trained as they should be? After an analytical review of the steps being taken and the activity of the individuals involved, assess what you can do to improve the process. Here it may be necessary to educate or change the personnel involved so that you can achieve your desired results.

Tweak To Improve

What if everything is going well? Don't be afraid to make it better than it was before. This is the time to try a few small tweaks to see what could work better. For example, you might try varying up your posting times here and there to see if you get better results.

Remember that your process is an ongoing mechanism, just like all the many processes that take place within your workplace every day. Get this one right and it can be highly satisfying to see people like, share, and appreciate your work. Get it wrong – well, then find out what you did wrong and make the fix as necessary.

And that's it! The five steps of running your social media enterprise. Now let's move on to a few guidelines to help you a little further down the road.

Section 4

The Six Golden Rules

We've set you up with the essentials for planning and implementing your strategy for success. Now it's time to look at a few rules designed to make your ongoing communications engaging. I call these the six golden rules.

Chapter 17

Be Creative

For some people, this is the fun part of the read. They're practically wringing their hands with glee. If you're one of them, then welcome! You're in good company. Creativity is indeed fun, in particular if you're the sort of person with a lot of unused ideas bursting at the seams.

If on the other hand you don't think you're very creative, it's fine. I've got some ideas on how you can approach your messaging and a few tips on what to avoid. Stay with me, it gets easier.

I think that by now we've all heard the complaint that no one wants to see endless pictures of people's pets, kids, or lunches. While we may have family or high school friends we've connected with through social media who commit those social faux pas ad nauseam, we've learned to block out their messaging. When their latest update comes through the feed, we scroll right on by. This is the same reaction your clients have to the bulk of the press releases and hacky advertising appeals that uninspired organisations release.

That's why it's essential to be creative. You still need to get your message out there, but in the process, why not make it appetising? Let's look at a couple of high profile examples of social media creativity.

The Old Spice Videos

In early 2010, the advertising agency Wieden+Kennedy dreamed up the "Smell like a Man, Man" ad campaign for Old Spice. Better known as "The Man Your Man Could Smell Like", the original ad starred a shirtless actor, Isaiah Mustafa, stepping out of a shower, walking onto a sailboat at sea, and then riding a horse on a beach all in one uncut shot. The original and imaginative campaign caught fire through social media. In the wake of those ads, there were 180 videos made, 5.9 million views, and 22,500 comments in less than a week. [7]

Old Spice responded directly to viewer comments through videos, creating what Visible Measures determined to be one of the fastest-growing online video campaigns of all time. The Old Spice responses video recorded nearly 6,000,000 views within the first 24 hours, nearly a million more than "Obama's Victory Speech", 1.5 million more than "Bush Dodges Shoe", and twice as many as "Susan Boyle".

There can be no doubt – making direct connections with your clients can boost your brand. While we can't all be Old Spice, nor do we necessarily need to aspire to their campaign's success, there is strong evidence that a creative, direct touch can influence and inspire your audience.

Campaigns like these also boost personal egos. There's something great about bragging rights. For people to say that they created a tweet that Old Spice personally responded to is

---

[7]   Ehrlich, Brenna, "The Old Spice Social Media Campaign by the Numbers", *Mashable*, 15 July 2010. Web, 23 May 2015

priceless. Who can tell how many lifelong product users this particular approach created?

The Zombie Apocalypse Comes To The CDC

Creativity needn't be limited to commercial campaigns. In May 2011, the United States Centers for Disease Control and Prevention (CDC) took a tongue-in-cheek approach to public outreach for disaster preparedness.[8]

> *Wonder why "Zombies", "Zombie Apocalypse", and "Zombie Preparedness" continue to live, or walk dead, on a CDC website? As it turns out, what first began as a tongue in cheek campaign to engage new audiences with preparedness messages has proven to be a very effective platform. We continue to reach and engage a wide variety of audiences on all hazards preparedness via Zombie Preparedness.*

In support of their message, the CDC launched a Zombie blog and a Zombie social media page with badges and widgets for other sites, along with ecards.

As of May 2015, the site is still viewable at the CDC's Office of Public Health Preparedness and Response.

On the surface, the storyline may seem to be that the CDC is cracking jokes about zombies. But does anyone think they aren't taking the job seriously? Hardly. Evidence shows that the creative message was the effective one. Consequently, they

---

[8]   "Zombie Preparedness", CDC: Office of Public Health Preparedness and Response, 10 April 2015. Web, 28 May 2015

accomplished their mission: getting people interested in real disaster preparation.

Sounds Great! Now What Do I Do?

What if you simply don't have the ideas on your own to make this sort of thing work? Hey, I said be creative; I didn't say it had to fall entirely on your shoulders. This is where drawing from an existing creative team or from your communications staff for ideas could be useful. Why not hold a little contest within your office for ideas to promote a topic? You could employ the internal social media platform to facilitate the idea creation and sharing process.

Any ideas suggested can then be fleshed out, chopped into a cohesive campaign, and disseminated across platforms at times that make the most sense. If you're coordinating traditional advertising with your social media, be sure you have a calendar with scheduled events appropriate to both.

When being creative, consider the potential fallout of a poorly executed campaign. Just because your idea sounds clever and fun, be aware that the general public may take it in a completely undesirable way. It's okay to road test these ideas by asking people to poke holes in the concept. It is, in fact, probably a good thing to include a checklist of steps taken to create a campaign.

Keep Your Eyes Open

While you need to develop creative solutions in order to get your message out there, you should be keeping an eye out on what's going on in the social media world already. You don't want to be a copycat, of course, but it's important to know what has already been done so that you can learn and develop your own ideas. Follow your competitors', industry leaders', and partners' accounts so you're keeping tabs on their progress alongside your own.

When you're pulling together the components of your creative campaign, ask yourself what you need to make it work. You'll very likely have to have the bulk of the campaign on a website and then point your social media back to it. It may not necessarily be the case, but a document or a website is the best way to provide a lot of information.

For the actual messaging, develop images, videos, and texts that are short and to the point. When you're looking at other people's creative ideas, ask yourself what drew you in. I can promise you it wasn't an incredibly long and complex concept, so simplify. Concise is best.

I mentioned images and videos, and I want to mention them again. You can certainly be creative with just a few words, but if you can tie in a short video clip or an eye-catching image, you'll have a much better shot at grabbing views.

Infographics Are Your Friend

Let's say you really need to get a more complex concept across to your audience. Maybe you want to educate them about a process or make an argument using some strong statistics. Concepts like these can be extremely difficult to share. A solution is at hand. Consider employing an infographic.

A good graphic designer can help you conceptualize your process or your ideas in an infographic form. Talk through your ideas with the designer and make it absolutely clear what you want to communicate. A strong designer may have some ideas about how to make that work; give them a listen.

Once you've settled on a design, supply the infographic designer with all the information you want to share. It's probable you'll need to map out any processes that need to be spelled out. Use very few words throughout the image; this will keep everything simple and easy to understand.

While infographics aren't as simple as a 140 character tweet or a paragraph on Facebook, they can be quite an effective way to encourage your audience to read and understand an idea.

Be Creative, But Be Effective

I hope you have a great deal of fun brainstorming and executing your ideas. Just be sure you don't fall so much in love with your ideas that you fail to communicate them.

One method of double-checking their effectiveness is to run them by the employees at the company. See what they think. It's possible that they will be able to poke some holes in the concept. If so, that's a good thing. It's better that you know any potential problems with the idea before you go public.

Chapter 18

Be Sharing

As I think we've well established by now, social media isn't all about you. It's social – it says so, right, in the name. Share your community's messages and they'll reciprocate.

We've already talked about how social media encourages the development of communities. If you're asking for something from your community through a call-to-action, you should expect to give back, especially to those who are your biggest supporters. An easy and greatly appreciated way of giving back is to share.

If material is being posted by another organisation that has a connection with your audience, it's fine to hit the share button. Your followers don't need to have an endless stream of materials that solely concern your organisation. The nice part of this is that while sharing is the right thing to do, it's also the effective thing to do.

When the time comes to share a crucially important message with a wider audience, there will be no stronger advocates on your behalf than the partners and friends whose own campaigns you've already championed. They can help get your message out to markets you wouldn't normally have access to, magnifying your content to a much higher degree.

However, sharing information and social media campaigns is just one element of sharing. While you want to increase your call-to-action effectiveness, there are other ways in which sharing can be mutually beneficial.

A key example: if you note someone has a question on social media and you happen to have the answer, you can, and should, respond; or, if you don't have the answer but suspect your followers and fans may have it, you can put the question out there for them to respond to. Let people know you need the help and they're likely to get back to you with an answer. This is a practice known as crowd-sharing.

What's more, if someone else has the answer, don't be afraid to get that word out on his or her behalf. People love it when they're retweeted and shared on social media. It shows appreciation for their expertise and it automatically credits the source of the material. Watch when it happens to you. Kind of an ego boost, isn't it? And why not? You are the best person to speak on the subject; you deserve the credit.

Sharing Information Is Power

There was a time, and I think we can both recall this fairly easily, when being a gatekeeper for information meant job security. If your primary purpose was to be the point person for a set of information, and be able to offer that information on demand, you had a job for life. At some point you'd naturally train a recent hire and mentor them for times you were out or for after you retired, but generally speaking that information wouldn't be shared with the entire office. You may even know a few co-workers who are still operating under the mental framework of keeping information.

There is data and personal information in the workplace that absolutely needs to be kept secure, but it must be said that keeping procedures to oneself is a sure-fire way of talking oneself both out of a job and into a failing workplace. Information wants to be free; set it free.

By sharing your information through appropriate channels, in particular processes and data that can safely be communicated with everyone, you are no longer a gatekeeper or a repository of exclusive information. You are a trusted authority and source for information. So long as you behave responsibly and provide the information your organisation needs to get things done, you are of value as a subject matter expert. Demonstrate your expertise by sharing internally when called upon without reluctance or fear of organisational change.

You've got your system well in place and you're watching your audience and interacting with them. Let's say you have a few followers and fans who are particularly good about sharing your information. When you have a campaign going, they're always the first ones on board with your game plan. They're your most supportive and vocal community members and you want to repay them for their loyalty. But how?

When appropriate, call them out with a thank you and engage directly with them. Let them know you are well aware and appreciative of their patronage. Simple acknowledgement through communication is a big reward on social media.

Of course, these folks have things to share as well. When appropriate, you may wish to retweet, share, and let other people in your community know about their messages. It may be that you can't personally endorse them, or that sharing could be seen as an inappropriate endorsement. If that's the case, by all means follow your organisation's policies, but if there's no conflict, be generous. The appreciation can result in a lot of opportunities in future.

If the organisation or individual in question is someone with whom it would be appropriate to do so, you could also make them part of your campaign. Share your tweets and posts in advance and let them pick and choose which messages they wish to share on their own platform. If they have time and interest, they'll be grateful you included them.

Share Responsibly

What do I mean by sharing responsibly? I mean avoid posting meaningless material. If there are partners who are creating material that's not relevant to your mission, or if you have a social media manager who isn't focused on your mission enough, be sure you're not diluting the purpose of your work. Your audience should be clear why they care about what you have to say. Give them what they want and expect. You'd want the same in your own experiences.

That's not to say you can't be creative with your message, as I've already suggested. Just make sure you're not alienating people by posting things that aren't factual. It may be eye-catching to post things that aren't always accurate, but that's only going to hurt your reputation. Don't do it.

There may be a temptation to share your materials with people who aren't part of your network. By mass targeting them with posts on their feeds, you're being counterproductive. It's never the right thing to share directly with people who don't want your information.

There are some unscrupulous folks out there who are peddling contacts: they claim they can give you thousands of Facebook fans or Twitter followers. The odds that any of them are real or helpful to you are minimal. It's not an overnight process to gain a big audience, but it's worth it.

Share With Your Eyes Open

Unfortunately, there are mistakes that people seem to fall victim to when they start off in social media. There are a few pitfalls I'd like to warn you about when it comes to sharing so you won't be one of them.

As you begin gathering information and sharing it, be careful that you're disseminating truthful information. Social media does rely upon the Internet as its backbone, and as we've all learned by now you can't believe everything you read on the Internet. The same is true elsewhere, of course, but the Internet has a way of coming across as convincing and truthful to many of us if we fail to do more than surface research. Don't be embarrassed by having to rescind untruthful materials.

Primary sources are absolutely necessary for any investigation, but a little simple research can also help you avoid looking foolish. Just because an image seems compelling and offers some information, you shouldn't take it as factual.

One trick I like to use: if you're not sure whether a message is fake or a hoax, copy the beginning of the message and paste it into a search engine such as Google or Bing. If the message turns up on a hoax-busting website (one of the better known ones is Snopes.com) you don't want to share that info!

What about quotes? Copy and paste. Often enough you can find out if the quote is accurate or not. Famous personalities are often found with their image next to a bit of text or reported statement that they never said. Be leery of sharing it without looking it up first.

There are other mistakes you may make as you go, but don't worry too much. So long as you are cautious and ask questions, you'll be fine.

Keep The Quality Level High

Get quality out of your social media and have great interactions by taking a moment, if needed, to think before you share that image or information. Is it information that is useful, timely, accurate, in demand, and what you'd want to see? Then you are all set to share, so share and be helpful to your community and network. Be a responsible, sharing part of your network and you'll enjoy the benefits.

Chapter 19
Be Timely

No one likes being the first one to the party. You know what's worse? Showing up after the party is all over. Set yourself up for social media success by knowing when it's right to speak and when it's right to listen.

Hint: it's most often the right time to listen.

Know How To Be Timely

The first rule of thumb for being timely is to let people know when you don't have all of the answers. It's fine to delay for a very short period of time if you let someone who's direct messaged you know that you're going to look into their concerns and get back to them. The important part there – get back to them. This will help your customers know what to expect from you while establishing a positive online reputation.

You can do this by setting the right expectations for responsiveness. If there's an information section on your platform, I'd recommend including the response time in the link you'll be providing to your policies. Let visitors know if there's not going to be any response time outside of normal business hours, during holidays, or over weekends. Though social media is always on, don't worry too much about this aspect; people know that you have a life and that businesses close during certain hours, so confirming their expectation is perfectly normal.

Incidentally, weekends are when spammers like to post on social media. You should probably plan to take a good look at your platforms on Monday morning, in particular if you plan to delete or block spam accounts.

After you've received a request for information, follow the work-flow that best processes and responds to the request within the timeframe you've noted. Your brand reputation will be enhanced by getting back to people with timely and useful information.

This process may involve a message moving from your monitoring social media manager to a subject matter expert and back again. If the information flow is moving slowly, the social media manager can let the requestor know that they'll be back in touch as soon as they have an answer.

Know When To Be Timely

Being timely in response to incoming requests isn't your only responsibility. You also need to be timely about getting your information out to your audience.

When being timely, it's a great idea to know the best times of day to post. That can be a moving target. Initially, I'd encourage you to do some web research and see what the latest numbers are during specific times of day for your particular platform. Usually, the best times to post will be around 9am, noon, and when people are starting to get home in the evening. Weekends can be bad, as I mentioned, but for a few platforms used to seeing a lot of weekend visitation that may be the prime time to post. Research on your own and test it out within your own processes to see what works best.

How should you do that? After you've used the Internet research as your guide, check out the analytics for each platform. The times of peak visitation (if this is something the metrics provide) may tell you a clear pattern that's particular to your presence. If you find posts repeatedly do best around 2pm, go ahead and post then. Always let your personal experiences in this department trump the suggestions of articles. You'll know what's best for you soon enough, if you pay close attention.

Now that we've figured out the times of day and the days of the week that work best, feel free to figure out how often you should post. You may want to prepare a number of tweets throughout the day for a particularly important message, given that the message dissipates over a very short period of time. However, with Facebook it might be better to post every day or every other day. It's a judgement call, and experience with each platform should help you decide the frequency.

The good thing about the time of day for posting internal social media is that it can be picked up by the audience at almost any time. So unlike external social media, I wouldn't put too much emphasis on which days and times you choose to post. It's true that you may do a bit better with a message around lunchtime or early in the day, but if you post close to 5pm on Friday, people won't be likely to see it until Monday when they come into work.

Dealing With Too Much Timeliness

If you know that on a specific day you'll be sending out many messages throughout the day for an event, let your audience know. For instance, if you expect to send out a lot of tweets during a specific conference, you may wish to give your followers a heads up so they can mute you for a day. Let them know it's a single day and encourage them to unmute when it's over. Be sure to tell them how long the event will last, or they may keep that mute button pressed permanently.

What about the over poster? The person who overshares on the internal social media channel, and it's not always useful information? You don't want to discourage people from using internal social media, but you do want the material shared to be appropriate to the workplace. If they're overdoing it, diplomatically suggest that they post a little more sparingly and cautiously, and be sure you're every bit as conscientious. This will ensure that their comments are seen and respected rather than automatically ignored.

Plan To Be Timely

Got the times, days, and frequency sorted out? Great! Plug that campaign into a social media calendar and stick to it. Be sure you schedule the messages and advertising to a time of year that makes sense. If your business is selling school supplies, you wouldn't advertise when students aren't in school. The same rules apply here.

To create a social media calendar, I'd recommend developing a calendar that includes each day you intend to post, the platforms you'll be using, and any details about your messaging that might be relevant. For instance, if you intend to put out a message on Easter, you'll want to note in your calendar the platforms, posts, and times. Ideally, there will be a particular reason you're promoting a message on that day.

Check the calendar on a weekly basis – I'd suggest Mondays as your ideal starting point – and update it by the end of each week.

Personally, I think the calendar can be laid out a year ahead, with updates planned as necessary for each new week you add. Of course, you won't necessarily have all the details a year out, but if you know a particular day is coming each year there's no reason not to note that in the calendar. And, of course, you'll want to keep an eye on the month and all upcoming weeks and events.

Coordinate the calendar with your communications team, making sure they understand that they'll need to develop their messaging in advance of the calendar.

When you post according to the calendar, this will help you maximise your campaign's potential. If there are sister organisations that could help you magnify the message, share your plan with them. Be sure to highlight those posts that will in some way reflect well on your partners. It'll make them more likely to want to share.

What if your social media person is out? If you have one person serving as your point person for messaging, I strongly encourage that you have a backup. It's a good idea in general. If that person were to leave on bad terms, you wouldn't want them to be the only one with the keys to all of your social media.

Now that you've got all your times, days, weeks, and months planned, you're ready to engage with social media in a timely fashion. You can schedule your posts, tweets, and other materials in advance using a scheduling tool. One of the more popular tools, Newz Social, allows you to both monitor and post in advance.

It can be quite handy to be able to set your message weeks ahead of the event, but be sure that any necessary changes are made in advance of the scheduled posts and tweets. It's easy to edit these messages. Check that your times are accurate as well.

If you're scheduling messaging for a different time zone, be sure to consult a time zone converter. It's possible that the time zone your scheduler has intended won't be the same as the one you're targeting, so plan accordingly.

There are still a few more areas we want to explore. After all, we did talk about technology early on. Brace yourself – it's time to talk tech some more!

Chapter 20

Be Tech Savvy

This chapter, simply by the name, may be the one which tempts readers to roll their eyes and heave a bit of a sigh. I started off the book by noting that the technical world can be a challenge for mature professionals, and I understand how it can be frustrating to have to embrace technology. Now I'm directly challenging you to "be tech savvy". What gives?

Like many industries within the information age, it's essential to be tech savvy when you're talking about modern communications. Because the necessity has been gradually working its way into communications, you may already be more tech savvy than you realise. Have you considered the extent to which you've already had to make adjustments to your way of thinking about organisational communications in the past 20 years? The transition from print to digital is so far underway that failing to keep up at all hasn't been a practical option for a decade. The computing power of the smartphone in your pocket compared to those clunky desktop computers of the eighties and nineties is overwhelming.

Don't worry, you'll get there. Do you know how you're going to do that? By practice.

The more you use a communications tool, the better you're going to get at it. Practice can make perfect, as they say. The same is true within the context of social media. Essentially all social media is a communications tool. The great thing about social media is that your active involvement in communities naturally fosters a mentoring situation – one that you can learn from and give back into.

Technology has to evolve constantly to keep up with the interactive needs of new generations. Even social media hasn't remained static. If you stuck by early popular favourites, MySpace and Friendster – two broad-based social media platforms that were once focused solely on connecting with friends and family, like Facebook – you'd now essentially be communicating on platforms that are focused on music and games, respectively. As of May 2015, the top 15 most popular social media platforms listed no longer included these two former juggernauts.[9]

So what are the most popular social media networks? According to that same listing, they are Facebook with 900 million estimated unique monthly visitors, Twitter with 310 million, LinkedIn at 255 million, Pinterest at 250 million, and Google+ at 120 million. And while those numbers may be true now, it's important to keep in mind that Google+ was launched four years ago and Pinterest five. It's impossible to say how long these five platforms will remain dominant and relevant, in particular as new innovators enter the marketplace.

This isn't a bad thing at all. While it can be frustrating to acclimatise to the newer entries in the field, they may also provide you with access to demographics you couldn't reach with the older models. What's more, you may find with experimentation that a specific social media platform isn't right for your business

---

[9]   eBizMBA, 1 May 2015. Web, 29 May 2015

model. Maybe a less popular platform is better for communicating with a specific constituency you need to connect with. That's something you can only determine for yourself after you've had a chance to test things out.

How do you keep current on what's going on? It needn't be a time-consuming process if you already subscribe to news feeds through news compilation sites like Google News, or you can use a content curation app like Newz Social to create your own news channels for your daily news reading. That will provide you with the latest updates and information, or at the very least, the high points. If you're looking for something more in-depth, you may want to check out a website with targeted information specifically discussing the latest trends.

Once you have an account on a social media platform, it's an excellent practice to pay attention to any notifications the platform owner may send out. Changes don't usually happen overnight, but may be phased in over a period of time. Some platforms frequently like to provide notifications in advance by sending you a direct email or by providing notifications on the site. Other platforms may be more likely simply to post the change and you'll discover it the next morning. That's why it's important to log into each and every account you own every working day.

You can also keep up on trends by talking with your peers online and through social media. This is particularly true with your *internal* social media presence. There's no reason why you can't have a section of your Intranet dedicated to discussing the latest trends in social media alongside your social media campaign discussions or any internal response coordination.

Internal social media can be a useful way of improving training and keeping IT professionals connected as well. When your IT department needs to provide vital updates to the rest of the staff, they can post updates through internal social media as opposed to simply sending out emails that are, unfortunately, all too often overlooked.

While your IT folks are talking through internal social media, consider using this as your own personal training opportunity. Encourage the creation of a blog for IT and/or social media providing internal updates. So long as the blog is topical and easy to follow through plain language, the entire organisation can take this as a learning opportunity.

If you are part of a larger organisation, consider returning to some older technology as a way to check-in and hold discussions. There's nothing wrong with hosting a coordinating phone call or conference call each month. You can also hold face-to-face meetings, perhaps even lunch meetings, for open discussion regarding policy and platform updates. If someone in your organisation is more comfortable with a specific platform (for instance, they may have personal experience working with an emerging platform that no one else has used), you may consider asking them to provide a presentation on their findings. For sole traders and small business owners, you can follow linkedin groups on social media tools to keep up to date with the latest know-how.

Why is it necessary to stay informed about these different platforms? Because, as I said, they're changing, and for the same reasons your industry changes all the time. Social media platforms want to compete with each other by offering better options. If one platform is deficient in some area, another will innovate. A newcomer may offer services the big players never thought of and practically overnight find itself at the top of the pack. It's certainly happened many times over the past few years.

While having to stay current can be a challenge, it can be its own reward. You'll never find yourself getting overly comfortable or bored with social media. The information flow is constantly changing on the feeds themselves, and you can use that to your benefit by subscribing to social media feeds that are informative. There's no shortage of social media accounts focused on the art of social media. If you have questions, ask away. That's why the experts are there to begin with. They want to field your questions. I should note, of course, the question may have already been asked, so don't be shy about using "search" before you ask.

As you're learning, your personal growth will expand and your value to the organisation will naturally increase. Staying relevant and trained is essential to keeping your career at the top of its game.

So don't be afraid of technology. It's definitely your friend. Before you know it, you'll find yourself fully tech savvy and ready to connect, regardless of your current level of technology comfort.

Let's change topics by talking about...well, topics!

Chapter 21

Be Topical

Imagine you're having a nice conversation with a friend about philosophy. Just as you're getting deep into the conversation, comparing the great thinkers and their systems of belief, what if a perfect stranger popped in and asked, "So, how about that football game yesterday?" You'd think they were mad or rude, or both. Yet people far too often do this exact thing on social media and think there's no consequence to their actions.

If you've ever had something like that happen to you, you're familiar with that unpleasant breed of annoyance. It's distracting, rude, and derails the conversation. The rules are no different on social media.

Like the irritating aunt who CAN'T HELP BUT TYPE IN ALL CAPITAL LETTERS online because she's not aware that it's considered shouting, you don't want to be seen as someone who wanders into a room and begins ranting on off-topic issues. Yes, you may have a product to sell. Recall that people like to buy things from people they support, not just the loudest and most frequent voice in the room. Lean into the topic that's being discussed and make that the point of your interaction each and every time so people don't ignore you, or, worse, block and boot you.

If you have an opportunity to speak with someone about a topic you're an expert on and you have the right forum to make your point, perfect. Carry on!

Spam isn't just a canned meat product. The whole world is familiar with spam email, and no doubt you have filters to keep you from unwanted communications in your own inbox. Be sure you're not spamming people's feeds with material that's not relevant to them.

As we talked about in Chapter 17, there are creative ways to get your message across. Be sure you're keeping your message and goal in mind. It's fine to ask questions of your audience and try to build up a good conversation, but there's no need to fill your business presence with a lot of unrelated materials. If you dilute your message too much, the people you hoped would select you for their feeds will begin to deselect you.

When you're involved in communities, remember that you're there to listen as well as speak. If you're not a subject matter expert on a topic, try not to present yourself as an authority. Instead, be open to learning more from those who are more informed. We may have more experience as mature professionals, but like everyone else we can't be expected to have expertise in all areas.

Another thing you may wish to do in order to stay relevant is to keep an eye out for days that are specifically tied in to your message. Holidays come to mind, of course. However, if your organisation is connected with a specific commemorative day or a major conference that's coming up, these are the things you can keep an eye out for. Have a great message ready and share when the time is right.

Speaking of conferences, we have yet to discuss how hashtags can work to your benefit. Sometimes discussions include a hashtag specific to a room where a presenter or group of presenters is holding a conversation. These are common events on Twitter. If you happen to be in the room, you might share your own thoughts on the hashtag.

There can also be virtual discussions revolving around a hashtag. While some hashtags may be frivolous, it's entirely possible to hold a meaningful conversation through a more organised Twitter "town hall". This is a situation in which one organisation manages a discussion over a hashtag while other organisations try to answer questions. It's possible some pre-written material can be developed for quicker responses, but overall you should be ready to jump in and act as a voice of authority.

Your internal media is an awesome place to be highly topical. Aside from the creation of single subject groups, you can hold town halls similar to the Twitter ones I've described. Let people know that you and a group of qualified experts on a subject (for instance, human resources, benefits, travel, etc.) are ready to answer live questions posted on the Intranet. Ways to handle this may include phone conferencing or being in the same room to coordinate incoming questions, setting a specific amount of time for questions to come in – for example, an hour. It helps to have a coordinator watching these conversations who can help steer questions to team members.

What if conversations on your normal social media platforms aren't going in a direction that you feel is productive? Of course, you want to try to engage with anyone who isn't "trolling" you; that is, trying to egg you into reacting in a bad fashion for the sole purpose of their own amusement. You should try to hold reasonable, pertinent conversations whenever possible.

The best way to get things back on track is to try to put things in the form of a question. For instance, instead of saying, "Our new website will be blue. Hope you enjoy it", you might say, "We're thinking of turning our website's background blue. What do people think of that?" If you're truly open to user interaction, you may get a good deal of useful information. Better yet, the time to ask the question may be when there are actual choices still in play: choosing between yellow or blue for your website's background colour, for instance. Having the social media folks weigh in may surprise you.

You might think such questions are a waste of time. Hardly. People love to be asked their opinions, especially if they have a strong opinion on a subject. The great thing about social media is that you're able to poll user experiences and opinions in advance of a project. It's particularly useful if the target audience on social media is connected to the topic at hand. They may not care which payroll system you use, but if your business is selling French fries, they may have very definite opinions about the type of oil you're considering using.

There's a slightly different approach you can take to this as well: simply link to a larger topic, such as a paper, and ask for public commentary. This is an effective way of letting your public know about a more complicated issue and making sure they feel both informed and that they have some say in policy. It's essential, of course, that their input be genuinely welcome and that you've made it clear that there's a cut-off for that policy discussion.

Above all, remember the message you're putting out is part of all your conversations. Do you really need to have that policy debate with the person who's poorly-informed and spoiling for a fight?

If it's not a productive, topical discussion, you have no business worrying about it.

How can you tell what's topical and what's not? That's a judgement call. You're probably used to making exactly that type of call every day in person, on the phone, or in meetings. If things are getting too far into the reeds, feel free to steer the discussion back to the point of the topic. If someone has personal concerns they want addressed, there are often more private conversations you could hold within the organisation or through an email.

I find topical discussions are extremely important within an organisation's internal social media. If someone wants to hold a political discussion and your business has nothing to do with politics, it may be wisest to explain that this isn't a good environment for that topic. You don't want to say no to everything, of course, but it can be clear at times when something is wrong for your group. Don't worry, you'll usually know.

Stay on topic within your social media conversations just as you try to do in your normal working day and you can't go wrong. It's okay to stray a little if it's in a conversational and fun way – we're all human – but overall it's generally best you stick with your strongest areas, and, importantly, the areas your community cares about. Don't be that guy, the one who babbles on and on about unimportant things. Your audience will respect and like you more if you listen and respond appropriately.

We've covered the respect you can earn for being topical. A final area we need to approach before we can be finished with our discussion is caring.

Chapter 22

Be Caring

We turn now to the final of our six golden rules. It may seem like an unusual topic to tackle, but being caring is an important aspect of being a social media guru. People know the difference between caring and pushing, and they don't react well to the latter. They tend to leave in droves.

Don't be a social media pusher! Instead, be the kind of person you'd want to spend time with.

What do I mean by pushing? There are social media users who view community members as nothing more than pawns for their own ends. I likened these communities to new markets earlier in the book; they're certainly that, but a market is made up of people first, not just sales numbers. Of course, we all have goals. That's natural, and people will expect you to have some ulterior motive for involving yourself in a social media community. The question is whether you are there solely to push yourself upon others or if you're willing to give and get. Do you actually care about any of the people you're interacting with? Then don't push.

Be Genuine

Caring isn't an area in which you can fake it until you make it. You either do care or you don't. If you don't, you've got a problem. Insincerity is easily detectable on social media, just as it is in other forms of communication. It's important to demonstrate that you care about the concerns of your audience and aren't just using them for your own means.

There are a few ways you can make sure you're being caring. For one, you should already have a good listening program in place. When you're listening, be sure you're clear on how the network members are reacting to you. At the same time, be attentive to what the audience is interested in. If they have something they want to hear more about, get back to them.

I'm sure I've said it a few times, but I find that ignoring people who have outstanding questions for you to answer is a clear indicator of a failing social media program. If you're responsive, you're caring.

When you do respond to people, take your time and think through what you need to say. Though you want to get back to them quickly, you are far better off if you're considering their point of view rather than just trying to make sales or connections, so avoid responding on the fly without thinking it through.

Be Sensitive To Your Audience

Thinking it through includes avoiding being insensitive. A social media audience is a global one, and there's no better way to turn people off than to speak insensitively, in particular if it's thought that you might be trying to take advantage of a situation for profit. The social media hall of shame is littered with individuals who were trying to build their brand at the expense of others.

This brings us to humour. Humour is wonderful. If you've got a naturally funny personality, that can be a huge asset on social media, but if you can't gauge how the things you say will be taken, you may want to pause before you push "post". Consider the number of professional comedians who've found themselves in hot water for an ill-considered remark in public or on social media. If it can be difficult for these professionals, is it a good idea for you just to say the first joke that springs to your head? Unless you're actually a comedian, you'd better check your efforts to be funny. The big questions to ask:

- Is my humour going to hurt someone else?
- Could I be viewed as unintentionally or, worse, intentionally hurtful?
- Is there any way what I say could lead to someone asking for my resignation?

Pause! If you find your post passes all those questions and you're still not sure, I'd skip it. You can, in theory, run it by some co-workers if you're really concerned, but I'd avoid that too. After all, if it's potentially offensive to the general public, it's potentially offensive at work. Use the same discretion you employ every day as a professional in this area.

As I said, humour is wonderful, and if you're good at it and don't think you'll hurt anyone's feelings, you're fine to go with it. In particular, if it's creative and can help you out rather than hurt you, go ahead and use it, but be careful.

Learn How To Agree To Disagree

One of the last things I'd like to share about caring is recognising the rights of your visitors to speak their minds freely. This can be a true issue with disagreements, a topic we covered briefly before but which deserves greater attention now.

It's okay to have discussions in which there are disagreements. However, these can be the trickiest of your potential social media engagements. We've talked a bit about what to do when an argument breaks out in your social media.

Realise that it's not always in your interests to argue on social media. You don't want to ignore conversations, but you should monitor them. You should adhere to any policies that require you to delete comments and warn users, but at the same time, don't be heavy-handed. Avoid banishing users from your social media unless it is absolutely necessary.

State policies as needed, but don't lower your professional standards by getting into petty arguments. Be thoughtful about the fact that others want to vent their opinions. Sometimes, they just want to make sure you're listening and understand their concerns. A policy change may be called for, and it's good to hear all sides. Just realise you can't please everyone all the time, but you can certainly respect their right to say what they need to say. It's possible that others will take your part anyway, so there's no need to say much.

Be Real With Real People

One of the hardest things to remember when engaging in online social interactions is the very real people behind the screens. For every thoughtless tweet or unpleasant interaction over Facebook, there's an actual human being on the other side who may be frustrated and simply wants to connect with you in a meaningful way. They may be bad at doing so, and perhaps they're carrying over some negative personality traits into their online persona, but they may not realise how they come across. Give everyone some slack.

When we interact with real people face-to-face, we have body language and facial expressions to help provide context. It is incredibly easy to misunderstand one another when we can't see each other or hear one another's tone of voice.

A pair of comedians did a skit in recent years[10] about two people chatting over text. One person is inviting their friend to come out for a drink. The friend misinterprets what they're saying and thinks they want to get in a fistfight. When the two meet, the second person arrives at the bar ready to kill the first, while the first merely orders a drink for the friend. It's a funny take on the embarrassing way we can easily misconstrue our intent without the usual personal interactions we take for granted.

Don't Feed The Trolls

I mentioned trolls once before, and as we close the chapter and prepare to end your training, I'd like to remind you who they are and how to avoid getting sucked into their negative feedback cycles.

Apart from not seeing the people you're interacting with, social media also provides a degree of anonymity that enables rudeness. You've no doubt already encountered this phenomenon. When you can communicate globally without the risk of meeting the other person, there are no social consequences for bad behaviour.

What does this mean to you? It means you're going to run into some jerks from time to time. Ignore them. Trolls enjoy pushing people's buttons until they become so upset that they eventually lose their cool. They do it for fun. While you want to give

---

[10] Key & Peele - Text Message Confusion   https://www.youtube.com/watch?v=HHL MXdDWD-o

your audience what they want, this is one of those rare occasions where you absolutely don't want to feed into people's comments.

When you run into such negative comments, there may be a tendency to feel bad about yourself. Why are these anonymous people harassing you and making you feel bad? It's hurtful and hard not to take it personally. I promise you, virtually everyone who interacts with the online world and through social media deals with negative comments. One late night comedian has even run a popular recurring skit in which celebrities read mean tweets about themselves.

Because it happens to everyone, I have to remind you to maintain a thick skin. As I said, everyone deals with it. Toughen up and ignore it.

That said, if you're really skilled at interacting with people, convert them. But whatever else you do, don't be drawn in by baiting and trolling efforts. It doesn't do a thing to make you feel better. You don't need to lower yourself to someone else's level, in particular when it's your reputation on the line.

Be patient, be respectful, and remember that the people behind the avatars are real people.

Go Forth And Conquer Social Media

Have I allayed your fears? Do you feel more confident about giving this new media technology a try? If the answer is yes, then great! I'm very pleased I could be of help.

Let's review the things we've learned in this book.

First, we talked about the reasons why you should use social media. Let's face it, if you don't believe it's going to help you out at your core, there's no reason to continue, right? Those steps include overcoming your fears, using social media as readily as you use your email account, and allowing people to connect with you via social media.

Once we'd reviewed the way it can help you build your business, I talked through a large number of common reasons you may be resistant to getting your feet wet. I tried to talk about as many of these topics as possible, and I think we can now agree the pros outweigh the cons.

After that, we dove into the building blocks of putting your plans into effect: the five steps of developing your new program. These five steps include knowing who your audience is and what you hope to get out of the effort; planning how you'd run the platforms; designing the program; analysing your work to date; and refining as you go along. If you execute these steps correctly, you'll have a system up and running before you know it. The processes should practically run themselves if you keep to the principles I've laid out.

We concluded with six golden rules, or the "Be"s, of social media: be creative, be sharing, be timely, be tech savvy, be topical, and be caring. If you keep those rules in mind and refer back to them often, you should be able to be victorious in your effort to be a social media champion.

If you still feel in need of training, check out online resources through some of the new communities you'll be plugging into or outsourced it to help you manage the professional side of your social media profiles.

Remember that you were new to all manner of technologies when you got your start, and over the years you've grown, adapted, and succeeded. This will be no different.

Every year, you change in ways you may not even realise. Adaptation is a part of survival and it's the key to having a happy life. If we stay inflexible, how can we ever develop? By reading this book, you've decided to make a concerted effort to communicate differently, to think differently, and to be a different you. Good for you!

Still not feeling super confident? It's okay. You're ready, really ready to get started. You've got this. Honestly, if you're still lacking in confidence, all I can say is give it a try. Perhaps start by studying social media more on your own, as we talked about in Chapter 4. Over time, I'm confident you'll overcome your concerns and fully engage in these opportunities. Trust me, it can be done. Mature professionals are excelling in social media every day.

I've given you all the basic tools you need to develop a winning social media strategy for your professional development with this. The rest is up to you.

Acknowledgements

I would like to thank my amazing team, Shawn Humphrey, Pat Gudhka, Yileen Koh, Jackie Reogo, Roshan Strange and Barry Watkins for their special magic of work that has helped me complete this book and still grow Curate Bee. I thank Peter Purushotma for his mentorship and support over the years. His generosity with his time to impart business knowledge to me is something I will always be grateful for. I thank the wonderful team at Newzsocial: Anand Jagannathan, Shastri Purushotma and Jeff Leroux for their guidance, support and wise words.

I would also like to thank Lucy McCarraher and her fantastic team at Rethink Press. Her expertise and experience have helped make this book even better than I thought was possible. I thank Andrew Griffiths, Glen Carlson and the KPI team for making my dream come true in publishing this book.

I thank the following friends who have helped me get through my challenging year with my cancer treatment and didn't say that I was crazy when I said that I was going to publish a book on social media this year – Susanne Harris, Donny Walford, Claudia Vaccaro, Rita Schade, Karen Roe, Mitchell Green, Dr Marcelle Freeman, Caren Matthews-Lane, Yvette and Mat Edwards, Nicki and Dan Watson, Peter and Carolyn Wilksch, Ruth Lawless, Alison Shaw, Dr Yasmin Darwich, Susan Jones and Dr Siwan Lovett.

Kate Teevan and Terri Baker for advising me to eat well so that I can still do what I love while going through my cancer treatment. I thank you for your research and nutritional information.

I am thankful for the Foreword that Steve Walker has written for this book. I am always at awe at his talents, enthusiasm and of course, his superior abilities of managing his social media influence.

I would also like to thank my wonderful sister, brother and mother, Sylvia, Steven and Lucy, who have given me their unconditional love and support and helped me with anything that I have asked for. They have been there for all of my life challenges and even more so for my cancer treatment while I was writing this book.

Lastly and most importantly, I would like to thank my husband Barry for bringing out the best in me since we met and for being a true partner in life. I am not a typical wife type, which he has never complained about but instead has shown his pride in my professional and personal accomplishments. His support is the real reason I was able to complete this as he took on more tasks to look after our daughter, who has severe physical disabilities, while I was going through the treatment and completing this book.

The Author

Sandra D'Souza started her professional life as an accountant but she took an unusual journey. Her focus was working in creative industries helping translate financial data into meaningful information for increasing revenue streams. Her 20 years of experience has spanned Sydney and London, where she was working in advertising, publishing and technology, including TV  corporations such as MTV Europe, EMI Records (UK), Telstra, Perot Systems and News Corp.

In 2012, she founded Curate Bee Digital, a digital marketing agency that brought technology, strategy and marketing together to deliver a unique suite of digital marketing services. Sandra lives and breathes all things business and has completed three university degrees including an MBA at Macquarie Graduate School of Management. She is also a member of the Australian Marketing Institute.

You can learn more about Sandra and Curate Bee Digital at:

Website: www.curatebee.com

Facebook: https://www.facebook.com/CurateBee

Twitter: @sandra_dsouza and @curatebee

Linkedin: https://www.linkedin.com/company/curate-bee

Google+: https://plus.google.com/b/1084312667317 49582209/

You can download #FreeBees content, tools and templates to help you gain an outstanding online presence that is authentically you from http://curatebee.com/freebees/